· BRITAIN ·
AND HER PEOPLE

Colour Library Books

This book is dedicated to Trevor Hall.

Design
Philip Clucas MSIAD

Commissioning Editors
Trevor Hall
Andrew Preston

Editorial
Jane Adams
Gill Waugh

Production
Ruth Arthur
David Proffit
Sally Connolly

Director of Production
Gerald Hughes

Director of Publishing
David Gibbon

CLB 2272
© 1990 Colour Library Books Ltd, Godalming, Surrey, England.
All rights reserved.
Colour separations by Scantrans Pte Ltd, Singapore.
Printed and bound in Spain by Graficromo, S.A.
ISBN 0 86283 786 3

· BRITAIN ·
AND HER PEOPLE

ANTONY KAMM AND CLAUDE POULET

~ Britain and Her People ~

FOREWORD

The problem confronting the British is that they sit plumb in the centre of their landscape and are therefore no more capable of perceiving the beauty surrounding them than the Mona Lisa would have been of understanding all the fuss about her smile. As regards the countless breathtaking beauties to be found in this book, we might pass by them every day, any day, and be too concerned with supposedly more important affairs to notice them. I myself, looking through the collection, have experienced pangs of self-reproach at the sight of spectacles I have brushed aside simply because I was too distracted by something else to stop and look. There was once a poet who asked the most telling of questions:

'What is this life if, full of care,
We have no time to stand and stare?'

In this invaluable volume, the eye of the camera stares on our behalf, creating unforgettable images.

I doubt if any publisher has ever gathered together between one set of covers a collection of colour portraits of Britain more perceptive, more moving, more beautiful than this one. Everything is here, from the broad, primary brushstroke of Trooping the Colour to the subtlest pastels of a moorland cloudscape. Inhabitants of this mad island who often wonder what it is that attracts so many millions of awe-struck tourists to its shores need wonder no more. All the answers are to be found in this memorable book.

Benny Green

Benny Green

Facing page: temporarily transferred from duties at the Tower of London, a beefeater stands guard at a Buckingham Palace garden party. Top: the commercial and domestic facades of village life. Overleaf: Chatsworth House.

INTRODUCTION

'O noble fool! / A worthy fool! Motley's the only wear,' exclaims the melancholy Jaques of his memorable meeting with Touchstone in Shakespeare's play *As You Like It*. If by 'motley' we understand not only a jester's clothes but also the word heterogeneous, then it precisely describes the extraordinary mixture of races and cultures that have come to Britain from over the seas and have stayed to impress their traditions and personalities on the land and its inhabitants. They began to come about seven thousand years ago and have been coming ever since.

When, in about 5,500 B.C., the forces of the Atlantic Ocean gathered strength and burst through the broad barrier of land which anchored the British mainland to the massive expanse of Europe and Asia, creating an island and thereby forging the destinies of England, Scotland, Wales and Ireland, Man's history had already begun. In Mesopotamia tribes had been growing wild wheat and barley, domesticating dogs and herding sheep, goats and pigs for several thousand years. They had built settlements, too, inaugurating a new civilisation in which people no longer moved from place to place foraging for food but had a home base. They could make laws, construct monuments to their dead and build altars to the spirits that they believed regulated man's existence.

The first permanent Britons, like the Mesopotamians, were farmers. By about 4,000 B.C. they were growing several kinds of crops and keeping cattle, as well as goats, sheep and pigs. They made pottery and used stone and flint implements to clear the forests and work the land and to fashion timber from which to build both houses and the intricate underground vaults in which they buried their family dead. Where stone was readily available, as it was in western Britain and in Scotland, this was used for building instead of wood. In about 3,000 B.C. a particularly intrepid band of farmers embarked with their families, cattle and sheep in wooden boats and sailed, or paddled, out into the unknown seas to the north of Scotland. They missed the island of Hoy and landed at Skara Brae on the western mainland of Orkney. Here they constructed an underground village complex from stone slabs, furnishing the cell-like dwellings with stone beds, tables and storage boxes and putting in individual drainage systems. Later Stone Age people were responsible for the vast stone monuments of which there are about nine hundred dotted around Britain. The most awe-inspiring and mysterious of all these is Stonehenge, which was a thousand years in the building. Amongst these people there arrived a new group, known as the Beaker Folk because of their distinctive drinking vessels. They brought with them a knowledge of gold, which was to be found especially in Ireland, and of copper, which they taught the native craftsmen to mix with tin from the mines in Cornwall to make bronze.

Facing page: modern day motley at the International Clowns Convention, Bognor Regis. Top left: contemporary druids celebrate the summer solstice at Stonehenge. Top right: the British weather – a rainy day on the front at St Ives, Cornwall.

While Bronze Age Britons were refining their craftsmanship, there was an upheaval going on in central Europe. Celtic-speaking peoples, having learned the secret of making iron and of forging it into all manner of useful and dangerous shapes, were now beginning to surge westwards with their fearsome new weapons. In about 750 B.C. they reached Scotland, where they combined with existing tribes to form, in due course, a new and somewhat mysterious race known as the Picts. Other Celts had taken over the east of England by the early fifth century B.C., and between then and the middle of the third century B.C. they implanted themselves in Ireland, Wales and the west of England. For the Romans, having a potentially hostile and possibly united nation living just beyond the boundary of their empire was both a grave risk and a challenge. In 56 B.C. they subdued the tribes of England and Wales, imposed their system of moderately benevolent imperialism, and embarked on a programme of road building, for efficient troop deployment, and domestic building, to house and entertain their officers and men. The Caledonians, as the Romans called the Scots, were finally left to their own devices, Hadrian's Wall having been constructed to keep them safely on the other side of this northernmost boundary of the Roman Empire. This was no doubt a wise move, as the Picts had been augmented by an even more warlike people who had emigrated to Argyll from Ireland. These men of Dal Riata became known as Scots, meaning 'raiders' or 'pirates'. The final retreat of the Romans from Britain was hastened by a hitherto unprecedented international alliance between the Scots from the north and from Ireland, the Picts and a new threat, the Saxons, from the European mainland.

There followed the period known as the Dark Ages. When the mists cleared, the Scots were attacking the Picts and Gaelic was becoming the language of Caledonia. Native Britons occupied the western lands of Britain, while Angles, Jutes and Frisians were settling in the eastern and central parts. The Britons referred to all these peoples as Saxons, which also gives the Gaelic word *sassenach* and the Welsh word *seisnig*. The descendants of these continental invaders called themselves simply Angles, or English, and the land England.

Above: old soldier. Distinctive red coats and black caps distinguish the four hundred Chelsea Pensioners, veterans whose privilege it has been since the time of Charles II to live in Chelsea Hospital. Facing page: young soldier – a Life Guard on sentry duty.

While the Celtic-based languages survived, and still survive, in Scotland, Ireland, Wales and Cornwall, the newcomers developed their Germanic tongue which, as Anglo-Saxon, is the basis of modern English. Then came the Vikings! These people from Denmark and Norway came first as pirates, then as conquerors and finally as settlers, accepting in due course the Christian religion of the people among whom they lived and adopting their language, which they enriched with words of their own.

By about 550, Anglo-Saxon kingdoms were being formed, first those in the east – East Anglia, Kent, Essex and Sussex – and then, as their armies moved westwards and northwards, Northumbria, Mercia, and Wessex. The Britons in the far west, whom the Anglo-Saxons called *welisc*, or Welsh, meaning 'foreign', resisted so fiercely that in about 790 Offa, King of Mercia, enclosed them behind a vast earthwork, now known as Offa's Dyke. This extended from the mouth of the Dee to the Severn Estuary, and its line still marks the boundary of the Principality of Wales.

In 843 the Picts finally capitulated to the Scots, and Kenneth MacAlpin became the first king of the combined territory of Scotia. He was crowned on the ancient Stone of Destiny and vigorously defended his new kingdom against Anglo-Saxon, British and Viking inroads. In 1018 Malcolm II, aided by the Britons of Strathclyde under their king, Owen the Bald, overran the English kingdom of Lothian. When Owen died the following year, Malcolm appropriated Strathclyde and installed his grandson Duncan as its ruler. The Kingdom of Scotland was now established.

Offa was in the habit of signing himself 'King of the English', but the first king who could truly regard himself as King of England was the Danish ruler, Canute. He formally assumed this title in 1017 after the murder of Edmund Ironside, who had, by agreement, retained the kingdom of Wessex when Canute subdued the rest of the country.

Above: one of London's Pearly Kings, who collect for charity in their spare time. Kersey (facing page top left) in Suffolk attracted Flemish cloth workers as early as the fourteenth century. Facing page top right: Welsh farmer, near Llanwrtyd Wells.

William the Conqueror took England by force, but the Normans entered Scotland by the invitation of David I, who died in 1153. The Welsh resisted until 1282, when Edward I's invasion tactics finally succeeded and Llewelyn II was killed at the battle of Irfon Bridge. The Normans introduced their system of government, which affected everyone from king to serf, and their architecture and they brought Britain into contact with political affairs and religious thinking in Europe.

The amalgam of Celtic, Anglo-Saxon and Scandinavian cultures which had been forged slowly over the preceding five hundred years proved much harder to alter than the system of government. The dialect of English spoken in the northern parts of England became, in the form later known as Scots, the language of the Lowlands of Scotland. With the establishment of printing in the fourteenth century, the dialect spoken in the southeast, the language of Chaucer, became the dominant form and the basis of standard English.

Immigrants since the Norman Conquest have contributed substantially to Britain's literature and other creative arts, to its economic and industrial structure and to its cooking habits! Jews were proscribed in 1290, but readmitted by Cromwell, after which they arrived in a steady stream from France, Portugal, and Spain, their numbers increasing dramatically towards the end of the nineteenth century and in the first half of this century as a result of racial persecution in continental Europe. For the same reasons, Flemish Protestants arrived in the sixteenth century and French Huguenots in the seventeenth, both communities involving themselves in the development of local crafts and industries. Irish emigration to the mainland was especially heavy in the nineteenth century, but the Irish have been exceeded in more recent years by those of Chinese, Italian and eastern European birth and by those from the younger nations of the Commonwealth, from the Caribbean, from Africa and from southern Asia. Yet, though there may be some fifty thousand new Britons each year, 1.2 million people left Britain between 1981 and 1986 to live abroad, only a few thousand less than were admitted into the country during that time. The mix may still be changing, but there are certain institutions and traditions that are now apparently enshrined in Britain and inbred into her people and are, as such, immutable.

~ *Britain and Her People* ~

· CHAPTER 1 ·

SPRING

'Spring, the sweet spring, is the year's pleasant king,' trilled Thomas Nashe. Besides the vegetation, spring brings a renewal of public spectacles, among which the band of the Grenadier Guards (above) is a firm favourite. For rugby players (below), spring marks the end of the season; for the salmon fisherman (right), it marks the beginning.

Spring

SPALDING BULB FIELDS

The town of Spalding in Lincolnshire lies about midway along that extraordinary corridor of rich, dark soil, some eighty miles long and ten to thirty miles broad, known as the Fens. This region of East Anglia stretches from Lincoln down to Cambridge, and from King's Lynn to Peterborough. Boadicea, Queen of the Iceni and scourge of the Roman army of occupation until her defeat and suicide in 62 A.D., ruled part of it. Later, Hereward the Wake, born and bred in the area, used the Fens as a base from which to carry out many of his most daring feats of arms, first against the Danes and then against William the Conqueror.

Most of Britain's agricultural areas were hacked laboriously out of the forest or scrub, which between them once covered the land, and were then diligently worked over by generations of peasants and landowners, each man concerned with enlarging, bit by bit, his own personal holding. By contrast, the Fens were reclaimed from nature by the exercise of hydraulic skills and the investment of large amounts of capital. For centuries the area had been a world apart, a

The predominance of tulips reflects the Dutch influence in the Spalding area whilst the more humble oil-seed rape, which now brightens many landscapes in Britain, offers a sharp colour contrast to the tulips and narcissi.

waterlogged morass of swamps and lagoons, dotted with oozy islands whose inhabitants eked out a damp existence by catching fish and snaring wild fowl.

The Romans were the first to begin the huge drainage operation, but theirs was a tactical rather than an agricultural measure, designed to cut across the region with canals, thus enabling corn to be more easily transported to the legionary fortress at York from the imperial estates in other parts of Britain and in the Mediterranean. It was Francis Russell, fourth Earl of Bedford (1593-1641), and his son William, first Duke of Bedford (1613-1700), who first saw the possibilities of copying in the Fens what had so successfully been done in Holland, to manufacture land from the pervasive marshes, watercourses and stagnant pools. The Bedfords brought over a Dutch engineer to make a survey, and, as a result of his

and cattle grazed over thousands of acres which only a few years before had been the sole haunts of geese, wild duck and bitterns.

Work continued throughout the eighteenth century in fits and starts, one problem being that the peaty earth shrank as it dried and, as a result, the land tended to sink below the level of the canals and drainage ditches. The building of hundreds of windmills to raise and remove the surface water only partially solved the problem, which had to be tackled further in the nineteenth century by the invention and application of the steam pump. Latterly, the layer of fertile clay just under the surface of the peat was dug up to fertilise the land or to supersede the peat as the topsoil. Today the Fenland region is one of the most fertile in Britain, and more than half the bulbs grown in England come from the part of it which lies round Spalding. Only at

report, they floated a company in 1630 whose subscribers, or 'adventurers', as they were called, were allotted a portion of the land to be reclaimed according to the amount of their investment. There was some opposition to the scheme from a local Member of Parliament and Justice of the Peace called Oliver Cromwell, and considerable resistance on the part of the Fenlanders, who for many years waged guerrilla warfare, destroying the dykes as they were built. Yet, in 1649, after the execution of Charles I, this same Oliver Cromwell supported an Act of Parliament to complete the scheme, the first stage of which was accomplished during the early years of the Commonwealth. Consequently, during Cromwell's rule as Lord Protector of England, crops were grown

Wicken Fen near Cambridge, a National Trust Nature Reserve, is the original nature of the Fens preserved. Ten miles away, the graceful might of Ely Cathedral rises like a mirage out of the flatness of the surrounding land, looking just as it must have to countless marsh dwellers during the Middle Ages.

The Dutch character of Spalding is evident in the architecture of the seven bridges across the River Welland. Amongst the town's historic buildings is Ayscoughfee Hall, once the home of Maurice Johnson (1688-1755), founder of the Spalding Gentlemen's Society, the second-oldest society in Britain to be devoted to literary antiquities and scientific research, and father, by his wife Elizabeth, of twenty-six children between 1710 and her death in 1754.

Picking the tulips for market. A tulip gatherer is depicted on Spalding's coat of arms, and over six million tulips are used to decorate the floats which take part in the annual Spalding Flower Parade at the beginning of May.

Spring

SOVEREIGN'S PARADE, SANDHURST

The men who defended Maiden Castle in Dorset against the Roman invaders in about 43 A.D. are the first British soldiers of whose exploits we know anything. Others fought with equal heroism against the legions of Agricola some forty years later. The men of Essex who so magnanimously allowed the Vikings to deploy on the mainland, before losing to them at the Battle of Maldon, were British soldiers, too. So were the Welsh and English archers who prevailed at Crécy and at Agincourt and the officers and men who fought so gallantly in the Low Countries in the latter half of the sixteenth century. The first regular British army, however, was that which paraded in its red coats in Windsor Great Park in April 1645. This was the New Model Army, founded by ordinance

Traditional emblems of office (facing page and top), the sword, sash, despatch case and staff, are carried or worn by those in positions of responsibility and command in the parade. Military bands, like the regiments they represent, have long, proud histories (centre left). Left: cadets facing the rigours of rifle drill as anonymous elements in a mechanical operation for the last time. The parade is as much for spectators (above) as for participants.

of Parliament at the instigation of Oliver Cromwell. Its first commander was Sir Thomas Fairfax (1612-71), who was replaced by Cromwell in 1650. On the Restoration of the Monarchy in 1660, some of its units joined the new royal standing army formed by Charles II, which served successfully under the Duke of Marlborough (1650-1722), under Robert Clive (1725-70) and under General James Wolfe (1727-1759). The army served with markedly less success in the American War of Independence, during and after

which its prestige plummeted. A more professional attitude to training was necessary. In 1741, the Royal Military Academy was established at Woolwich to train cadets to become officers in the Royal Artillery. The establishment of a training college for officers in other army units was the brainchild of the Guernsey-born Lieutenant Colonel John Gaspard Le Marchant (1746-1817).

In 1797, Le Marchant was serving in the 7th Light Dragoons in Windsor, and had already devised a form of cavalry sword exercise that was being adopted by regiments in the British Army. To carry out his ideas on training, a suitable house was taken in High Wycombe, Buckinghamshire, and General Francis Jarry (1733-1807), a French emigré, was invited to deliver lectures on military tactics. Jarry soon concluded that the general educational standard of his pupils was not high enough for them to benefit properly from his instruction, and further teachers were appointed in mathematics and fortifications. Le Marchant now submitted proposals for a national training establishment to the Duke of York and Albany (1763-1827), second son of George III and Commander in Chief of the Army. The Duke's organisational abilities and reforming zeal were never in doubt, but his lack

Drill masters ensure the parade goes like clockwork, each soldier fulfilling his role perfectly. The advent of the new-style, shorter rifle means that, even when momentarily at ease (below), the soldiers cannot rest the rifle butt on the ground. Traditionally, the adjutant of the parade exits by riding up the ceremonial steps (bottom left).

of judgment in more personal matters led to his resignation as Commander in Chief in 1809, when it was discovered that his mistress, Mary Ann Clarke, was taking money from officers and then using her influence, and charms, to gain their promotion. With the Duke's encouragement, the new training school was given semi-official status in 1799, and in 1801 Parliament granted 30,000 pounds for the formal establishment of the Royal Military College. It had a senior department at High Wycombe, with Jarry as Commandant, and a junior department, to train cadets for commissions in the cavalry and infantry, in Great Marlow, where William Harcourt (1743-1830), later Field Marshal Earl Harcourt, was appointed Governor, and Le Marchant Lieutenant Governor. During their nine-year stint, over two hundred officers passed through their hands, and there is much evidence that Le Marchant's initiative, combined with the other reforms of the Duke of York, contributed greatly to the efficiency and effectiveness of an army whose finest hour was on the field of Waterloo in 1815.

Left: the eyes right manoeuvre is facilitated by the ingenious distribution of men of different heights. Female officers (below) have been trained at Sandhurst since 1981. Hats are de rigueur for the spectators, too, and even casualties must wear full dress uniform.

In 1812 the junior department moved to Sandhurst, into what are now called the Old Buildings. These were designed in ducal style by the architect James Wyatt (1746-1813). The land on which they stand was purchased for the purpose by the Prime Minister, William Pitt (1759-1806), from his own niece. The senior department moved there a few years later, becoming the Staff College in 1858. The purchase of commissions was abolished in 1871, but the Royal Military College continued to train 'gentlemen cadets' for the cavalry, the infantry and the Indian Army until the outbreak of World War II in 1939.

In 1947 the Royal Military Academy and the Royal

Military College were combined, and the resulting establishment was reopened as the Royal Military Academy, Sandhurst. Since then the Academy has trained over twenty thousand officer cadets and student officers, including overseas cadets from more than sixty countries. Today there are separate courses for non-graduate, graduate and female cadets, at the successful conclusion of which commissions are granted to non-graduates and confirmed for graduates. The annual Sovereign's Parade, in which over five

Top: on a day that belongs to the military, the traditional City uniform looks out of place. Top left and far left: Major General HRH The Duke of Kent, representing the sovereign at the parade. Above and left: a representative of the Brigade of Gurkhas from Nepal, a reminder of the far-flung nature of the British Army.

hundred student officers and officer cadets take part, marks these events. The Sovereign's Banner, presented to the Academy in 1974 by HM the Queen, is carried by the champion company, which is known as the Sovereign's Company. The Sword of Honour is awarded to the best member of the graduate course, the Sash of Honour to the best woman cadet, and the Queen's Medal to the most outstanding participant in the military and practical tests.

Instruction at the Academy is in leadership, tactics,

the army. Maps will be interpreted in exactly the same way by every officer. Orders will always be given in certain sequences, to ensure their immediate comprehension. Of course, no approach which is largely academic can compensate for actual war experience, but an understanding of the strategic, economic, and sociological background to a conflict may lead to a general discussion on the nature of war and to a clearer view of the formidable factors raised by that inevitable question, 'What is it like to be in

Below left: past military encounters with England forgotten, two officers of a Highland regiment, in their distinctive uniforms, take a front seat at the occasion. Below: the adjutant commands the parade from his charger, Blitz.

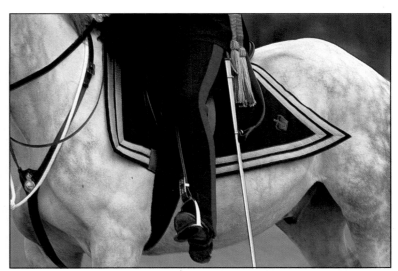

As they march off the parade ground at the end of the ninety-sixth Sovereign's Parade, the 535 participants (left), over half of whom are graduates, have now either become officers or had their commissions confirmed. They will soon be joining their regiments or receiving further instruction in specialist skills. From being at the mercy of their drill sergeant (above) they will now belong to that elite group, the officers of the British Army.

map reading, signals, skill at arms, drill, administration and organisation, as well as in academic subjects. A certain amount of character moulding is indulged in, to ensure that the standards of general behaviour expected of an officer are properly understood, and that those distinctions between officers and other ranks which are held to generate respect towards an officer are either implanted or maintained. The interminable rounds of parade-ground drill and arms practice have their purpose, too. The development of automatic responses, together with standard procedures and forms of expression, enable events and situations to be assessed quickly and described in terms which will be instantly recognisable throughout

battle?'. For even in peacetime, officers and soldiers may find themselves under fire in Northern Ireland or, as in 1982 in the Falkland Islands, fighting several thousands of miles away, or serving as members of a peace-keeping force anywhere in the world.

Sandhurst is a military establishment, run by army officers on army lines. Yet the cadets are as often to be seen in civilian clothes as in uniform, looking like any other group of students, if rather neater and more tidily dressed. One of their permanent number, however, is always in uniform. He is Senior Under Officer Edward Bear, a genuine and venerable teddy who certainly knows the ropes, having accompanied cadets on parachute drops for over twenty years!

Spring

A WELSH SPRING

Wales is a country of mountains and deep valleys whose landscapes are some of the most spectacular in Britain, as well as, industrially, some of the most depressing. The Welsh themselves can no more claim to be a racially pure nation than can the English or the Scots. All three countries have received, and often benefited from, waves of invaders and immigrants from prehistoric times onwards. As a people, the Welsh are more fiercely nationalistic than the Scots, and more possessive of their own language, yet Glamorgan has to play in the English County Cricket

In the rural fastnesses of Wales live the hardy individuals who earn their living from this beautiful, yet sometimes hostile, countryside. Eighty per cent of the land is devoted to agriculture, mostly sheep, cattle, or dairy farming. Top right and above: farmhouse at Llanerchymedd, Isle of Anglesey. Centre: Pass of Llanberis.

Championship and Cardiff City, Swansea Town, and Wrexham in the English Football League. However, whereas the five million inhabitants of the officially designated Kingdom of Scotland have, since 1603, accepted, though not always unanimously, the monarch of England as their own sovereign, Wales, with her population of two and a half million, is a principality. Since 1301 she has had the right, though not an automatic one, to have her own royal prince.

In Wales, the Romans achieved against the native

Left, below and bottom left: sheep roam the fresh spring pastures. Even the most idylllic valley can reveal a face scarred by commercial exploitation, as in the Pass of Llanberis (far left). Bottom: the old mill at Dyfi Furnace exhibits cracks in its walls beneath a new slate roof.

Celts what they were never to achieve against the inhabitants of Scotland: by about 80 A.D. they had subjugated them all. Yet, when the combined attacks of the Picts and Scots from the north, and the Saxons from the east, began to topple the power of Rome in the fourth century, it was a Roman soldier, one Magnus Maximus, who, under the Welsh name Maxen Wledig, was the legendary founder of the Welsh dynasty of Gwynned, which lasted until 825. Whether or not this is true, Magnus Maximus did proclaim himself Emperor of Rome in 383, was accepted by the army in Britain and, after crossing over to Gaul, ruled the western provinces for five years, until he was defeated and killed in Italy whilst attempting to best his rival for the imperial throne. The Welsh were left hemmed in by hostile tribes and, when the Romans finally abandoned Britain, the Saxons poured in. In 577 they isolated the Welsh from Cornwall, and, in 613, effectively cut them off from their compatriots in Strathclyde and other parts of the north. This is the period of King Arthur, the semi-legendary leader associated with the British tribes which had been driven back into Wales. He is said to have fought twelve great battles against the Saxons, culminating in that of Mount Badon, in which he 'carried the cross of Our Lord Jesus Christ on his shoulders for three days and three nights and the Britons were the victors', and 'nine hundred and sixty men fell in one day from one charge of Arthur, and no one overthrew them except himself alone'. This is quite some achievement, even in heroic legend, but Badon was a real battle, which probably took place in 518. In the

was Llywelyn ap Grufydd. He died in 1282 fighting the English troops of Edward I, whose policy was to hammer the Welsh as hard as he later tried to hammer the Scots. Llywelyn's head was stuck up outside the Tower of London, where it was joined by that of his brother, David, who had been handed over by 'men of his own tongue', a fate which was suffered twelve years later by the Scottish patriot, Sir William Wallace. Both David and Wallace were dragged by horses to be hanged, and were then drawn and quartered. By the drastic Statute of Wales in 1284, the Welsh lost their independence. They retained, however, their passions, traditions and language, and they got another sovereign prince. This was by way of a public relations coup by Edward I who, promising the Welsh a native-born prince who 'could not speak a word of English', then showed them his infant son, later Edward II, who had, conveniently, just been born in Caernarvon. His appointment was not confirmed until 1301.

Today just under twenty per cent of the population of Wales can speak the Welsh language, and, since

Snowdonia (below) covers 854 square miles and is one of ten areas of untamed and spectacular countryside in England and Wales that have been designated national parks. Snowdon itself, at 3,560 feet, is the second highest mountain in Britain, after Ben Nevis.

eighth century, the Welsh found themselves further beleaguered by Offa, King of Mercia, who made inroads into their territory and then protected his acquisitions by constructing a 150-mile-long dyke from the River Dee to the River Wye. The Welsh had no option but to accept this as a new boundary. The first recorded king, or sovereign prince, of all Wales is Rhodri Mawr, the only ruler to bear the sobriquet 'the Great', who ruled from 844 to 878. His grandson Hywel Dda, the only one to be called 'the Good', ruled from 916 to 950 and was responsible for codifying the laws of his nation. A hundred years later, the Welsh were once again fighting for their survival as William the Conqueror's Norman barons made inroads into their territory. The last native Prince of the Welsh

A brightly painted farmhouse nestles in the lee of a hillside in the Pass of Llanberis, one of two picturesque passes running through the mountains of Snowdonia.

the Welsh Language Act of 1967, legal proceedings may be conducted in Welsh and 'England' is no longer automatically assumed to include the land of Wales in Acts of Parliament. The Welsh linguistic tradition has been maintained only with difficulty, and any privileges have been obtained by long campaigning. Ironically, it was under the Tudor dynasty of English kings, founded by a Welshman, that English became the official language of Wales. Owen Tudor, his anglicised name, was a page to Henry V. One day soon after Henry's death, his comely young widow, Catherine de Valois, discovered Owen bathing naked. The attraction was mutual, and their affair blossomed into marriage. Owen's grandson, Henry VII, became the first Tudor monarch, and it was his son, Henry VIII, who promulgated the Acts of Union of 1536 and 1542 which gave Wales and England equal rights under the Crown, with this one vital snag: 'No Person or Persons that use the Welsh Speech or Language shall have or enjoy any Manner of Office or Fees within this Realm of England, Wales, or other of the

King's Dominion, upon Pain of forfeiting the same offices unless he or they use and exercise the English Speech or Language'. The message to those Welshmen who wanted to get on in the world was, 'bilingualism or starvation'. Yet Henry's motives were those of statesmanship rather than of blind imperialism. He wanted to appear on the European political scene as king of a single nation with a single official language. That Welsh survived, even in the face of the 1870 Education Act which made English the medium of instruction at primary level, was due to the sixteenth-century Reformation, which made the Bible and the Prayer Book available to every person in their own

tongue; to the publication of a Welsh grammar and dictionary in 1621 and 1632 respectively; to the spread of the Methodist movement in the eighteenth century and to the strength of the Welsh literary heritage. From the bardic tradition whereby every court, whatever its size, had not only a master poet, who recited to the more superior members of the household, but also a junior poet for the rest, there came a wealth of stories. Eleven of these were first written down in the fourteenth century and later put together as *The Mabinogion*, a gloriously diverse collection of ancient folklore, with Romano-British, Celtic, and Arthurian overtones. Medieval Welsh

When his flock are scattered over a wide area or rough moorland, a hardy, native pony (top right) is the sheep farmer's best means of transport. Top Left: Llanwrtyd Wells Church, Powys. Centre: the house of Welsh poet Dylan Thomas looks out over the bay of Laugharne (above left). Above: a splash of red amidst the green of the moors near Tregaron.

Moments of relaxation (left) are few and far between for a farmer, so enjoying them to the full is a must. Below left: a simple wooden cross marks the grave in Laugharne churchyard of the best-known and most popular Welsh poet of the twentieth century. Below: a farmer instructs his sheepdogs in time-honoured fashion.

poetry is best represented by Dafydd ap Gwilym, a very worldly cleric who, by his own account, could not take his eyes off the women, despite little success. The annual Royal National Eisteddfod, an eighteenth-century revival of a genuine medieval tradition, conducted entirely in Welsh, is today the focus of Welsh folk music, singing, and poetry. The climax of this colourful exhibition of pomp and ceremony, presided over by an Arch-Druid, is the naming of the Bard, the winner of the year's poetry competition. The new Bard is then chaired from the platform in an elaborate wooden throne, specially carved for the occasion, which he takes away with him.

Paradoxically, the most famous and internationally popular Welsh poet of the twentieth century knew no Welsh, though his musical poetry and verbal extravagances are essentially Welsh in character. Dylan Thomas, outwardly a ranting, roaring drunk, but at heart a gentle soul, was a poet, and also a prose writer, of great feeling and originality, who died in New York of alcohol poisoning in 1954. He was only 39. After an undistinguished academic career at Swansea Grammar School and an early job as a reporter, he became a professional poet. The first of his poems to appear nationally was published in 1933 by the *Sunday Referee*, which awarded Thomas its major literary prize and financed the publication of his first book, *18 Poems*, in which the authentic voice of a frustrated teenager speaks. Among his most accessible poems are several of a celebratory, nostalgic nature, including *Poem in October*, *Poem on his Birthday*, *Fern Hill*, and *In the White Giant's Thigh*. *Under Milk Wood: a Play for Voices* is still frequently performed. The poet's Welsh home on the coast at Laugharne is preserved as a museum.

The Welsh, as anyone can observe, are born storytellers, actors, and singers, and excel at most things, including Parliamentary debates and forensic oratory, which call for a degree of flamboyance and a sense of drama. Nowhere are these two things,

together with the patriotism of the Welsh, more evident than on the rugby football field. Rugby came late to the valleys and coastal areas of south Wales, but it quickly caught on as a modern version of the folk-football game 'cnappen' and flourished with an intensity unmatched elsewhere. This was reinforced in the 1880s by an influx of immigrant workers from the west of England and from Ireland, where association football had not yet been firmly established. Rugby football unified the Welsh people because it was a democratic amateur sport. Brawny miners and

powerful policemen packed down with and ran alongside doctors, lawyers and others from the grammar and public schools. These men were forged into teams which took on, and often beat, the world with their unique blend of inspiration, passion, and physical strength. The spirit and the tradition still burn fiercely. In September 1989 the President of the Welsh Rugby Football Union, having resigned on a political issue and then been persuaded to reverse his decision, summed it up: 'When you are involved in Welsh rugby, it is something more than life itself.'

Rugby has always been a great source of Welsh pride, and rugby pitches are squeezed into any available space (top left) to accommodate the many local clubs (top). This enthusiasm and competitiveness are apparent even at youth level (remaining pictures).

Spring
LLOYD'S OF LONDON

Lloyds of London, the most famous insurance organisation in the world and one of Britain's biggest financial institutions, was set up three hundred years ago as an extension of the services offered by a London coffee house. It has retained its unceremonious nature ever since. Marine insurance is known to have been introduced to Britain in the sixteenth century by Lombard bankers, but its origins go back to the first century A.D., when Claudius, Emperor of Rome, undertook to indemnify grain shippers for losses sustained on the open sea. Edward Lloyd's claim to fame is that he provided the premises and facilities in which his clients could conduct their marine insurance business, and published reliable information about those ships which had sailed from or returned to the sheet of folded paper which outlines the risk. An underwriter's signature on the slip is binding. Since the 1880s, policies have been extended to cover risks other than ships and their cargoes. As well as insuring properties against fire and burglary and providing cover against motor and, from as early as 1911, aviation accidents, Lloyd's is now involved in space technology and communications satellites. The first salvage mission in space was financed by Lloyd's underwriters. These same underwriters will consider even more unusual risks. Thus, a famous distillery was able to take out a policy against the live capture of the Loch Ness monster, for which it had offered a prize of one million pounds.

those ships which had sailed from or returned to Britain. Lloyd died in 1713, but his *Lloyd's News* survives as *Lloyd's List,* as it was renamed in 1734. Lloyd's is not a company, but a society, incorporated by Act of Parliament in 1871, which is secured by thirty thousand private individuals, each being the nominee of one or more existing members, and, as underwriters, pledging their entire personal fortunes. Since a further Act of Parliament in 1982, the society is governed by its Council, comprising sixteen working and eight external members. Members are represented on the market floor by 370 syndicates, each spearheaded by an 'active underwriter', or insurance specialist, who works from his own 'box'. He considers risks offered by accredited brokers, who are in turn acting for clients requiring insurance cover. The syndicates are in competition with each other, and a broker may obtain a few premium quotations before making his choice, or he may spread a large risk by approaching several syndicates to complete his 'slip',

The unusual design of the modern Lloyd's building (these pages), which opened in 1986, satisfies the requirement that all the underwriting business should be done in a single room – a survival from the days of Edward Lloyd's coffee house. The famous Lutine Bell (centre) was raised in 1859 from the wreck of HMS Lutine, lost in 1799 with all hands and a valuable cargo insured by Lloyd's. The bell is rung whenever an important announcement affecting the market is to be made. Two strokes indicate good news, and one that the news will be bad.

Spring

THE GRAND NATIONAL, AINTREE

As early as the reign of Henry II, horse races were held in Britain, usually at Smithfield, which was the principal horse market. The public, however, preferred tournaments and jousting, and so racing lapsed in favour until the time of James I, who built racing stables by his palace. Charles II was also a devotee of the races, particularly at Newmarket, where they had been held since the 1640s. By the middle of the eighteenth century, horse-racing had become established as an organised sport. The Jockey Club was established in 1752, and this was followed by the founding of the three classic flat races, the St Leger (1776), the Oaks (1779), and the Derby (1780). In 1752, two Irish hunting men named Blake and

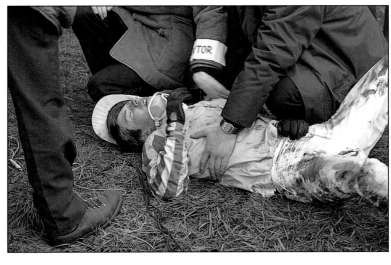

O'Callaghan challenged each other to race across country between the church steeples of Buttevant and St Leger. The distance, significantly enough, was four miles 855 yards, the length of the present Grand National. The term steeplechase meant exactly that; races were run between church steeples, which were easily identifiable and could be kept in sight. The race went to the horse and rider who rode most quickly and most directly between the two steeples, jumping all natural hazards encountered on the way: fences, hedges, ditches, and brooks. The first public steeplechase was held at St Albans in 1830. The Grand National Steeplechase, Britain's premier race under National Hunt rules, was first run over two miles at Aintree, near Liverpool, on 26 February 1839, when it was called the Grand Liverpool Steeplechase. The crowd of over fifty thousand was so unexpectedly large and excitedly uncontrollable that the stewards had difficulty in clearing the course for the start, which was delayed for two hours. Even so, when the 'off' was called, one horse, the Irish-trained Rust, was still

lost among the spectators. Out of seventeen runners, the first winner was Lottery at 5-1, owned by a Mr Elmore and ridden by the dapper Jem Mason.

The race was renamed the Grand National in 1847. Early crowds were not interested solely in the racing. In 1871, police broke up a cock-fight on the course, and in 1875 they arrested two prizefighters. In each case the link with horse-racing was the additional opportunities these activities offered for betting. In 1843, the owner of the course, Edward William Topham, turned the race into a handicap, and so it has remained ever since. The handicap is applied by adding weights to balance that already carried by each horse, in the person of its jockey, so that, theoretically, all the horses have an equal chance and the outcome should be a dead heat. In practice this is never even the remotest of possibilities, as the course is four miles 855 yards long and thirty of the most formidable fences in the world of racing have to be negotiated en route.

The fences are constructed of thorn and topped

The Grand National attracts many serious racing fans (facing page), but even deep concentration cannot guarantee picking the winner. Between the relative calm of the paddock before the race (above left) and excitement of the run in to the winning post (top left) there are many thrills and spills to observe. Although falls (above) are commonplace, serious injuries to jockeys are rare. For the winning owner (top right) there is the added bonus of receiving the trophy from HRH the Princess Royal.

with spruce. Some of the thorns are allowed to take root, creating a partly natural hedge historically related to the hazards of the original steeplechases. The fact that each fence is three feet wide and between four feet six inches and five feet two inches high is enough to deter any apprentice rider or inexperienced horse. In addition, five of them have either an open ditch in front or a brook behind. The most fearsome fence is known as The Chair and is jumped only once on the double circuit. It consists of a yawning six-foot open ditch followed by a five-foot-two-inch fence, and is all the more terrifying for the riders because it is

immediately followed by Valentines, a five-foot fence with a five-foot-six-inch brook on the other side. The most fiendish fences are not always the most disastrous. It was at the simple four-foot-six-inch fence immediately after Bechers Brook that most of the field tangled and fell in 1967. The 100-1 outsider, Foinavon, was so far behind at this point that he missed the mayhem, his jockey was able to steady him enough to jump clear of the fallen horses, and Foinavon won the race at a canter. The fence now bears his name.

Out of the many entrants for the race each year, about forty actually come under starter's orders, and

Hats, from the jaunty trilby of the serious punter (far left) to the elegant headgear of the serious lunchers (left), are a feature of race meetings everywhere. Below left: HRH the Princess Royal, herself a licensed jockey, unveils a life-size bronze statue by Philip Blacker of the legendary Red Rum to mark 150 years of steeplechasing at Aintree. Red Rum himself, now a spritely 23-year-old, seems more interested in the platform party than in his likeness. Jockeys and owners get a chance to chat (below), standing in the paddock before the race.

immediately in front of the stands, where the crowd is roaring, and because it is only half as long as the other fences. The most notorious fence is Bechers Brook, so called after an incident in the very first race in which a Captain Becher parted company with his horse, Conrad, and was deposited in the water. The fence's difficulty lies in the fact that it is immediately followed by a steep drop and the first left-hand turn of the race. Thus, as the field approaches the fence for the first time, riders are jockeying for a position on the inside, a risky manoeuvre. The bend at the five-foot fence known as the Canal Turn is even more pronounced, being virtually a right-angle, and it is

lad. An additional prize is awarded to the stable lad in charge of the best-turned-out horse.

Whilst there is no limit to the number of times a horse can run in the race, which is now confined to horses of seven years and upwards, only four horses have won it twice running: Abd-El-Kader in 1850 and 1851; The Colonel in 1869 and 1870; Reynoldstown in 1935 and 1936; and Red Rum in 1973 and 1974. The extraordinary Red Rum won it again in 1977, and was second on two other outings. Of all the remarkable, and romantic, finishes and finishers, Bob Champion and Aldaniti in 1981 take the palm. In this winning combination, the jockey had been a victim of cancer and the horse had only just recovered from severe leg injuries. The race is also about trainers and owners. M.V. O'Brien trained the winners of three consecutive races between 1953 and 1955. Mrs Jenny Pitman was the first woman to train a winner with Corbiere in 1983. When the third favourite, Door Latch, crashed at the first fence in 1986, it was thought that with him went his ninety-year-old owner, Jim Joel's, last chance to win the Grand National. Yet the very next year, his horse, Maori Venture, ridden by Steve Knight, caught up with the leaders at the last fence and galloped away up the final, agonising stretch to win. At the time, his owner was in mid-flight, returning from his South African homeland.

Above left: dejection speaks volumes. Above: elegance and a copy of the Sporting Times *breed confidence.*

the winner will cover the course in between nine and ten minutes, depending on the state of the ground. Jumping a clear round is such an achievement in itself that the Aintree Clear Rounds Award was instituted in 1986 for jockeys who have done this five times. The record is nine times, by David Dick. Finishing the course is also regarded as something of an achievement. The first woman jockey to compete in the race was Charlotte Brew in 1973. Unusually, there are prizes for the first four horses. The winning owner receives the Challenge Trophy and a sum of over 50,000 pounds, and there are also trophies and prizes for the winning trainer, jockey and chief stable

Spring

EASTER PARADE, BATTERSEA PARK

In the leafy coolness of Cheyne Row, Chelsea, still looking much as it did when he died, stands the home of Thomas Carlyle (1795-1881), dour Scottish philosopher, critic and historian. At the bottom of the street, in the middle of a wedge-shaped bit of green, sits the philosopher himself, in his dressing gown. He is gazing, with a pensive and slightly quizzical air, across the sluggish river to Battersea. The immediate prospect is of a row of low, industrial-type outbuildings beside a series of weird constructions put together with seeming haphazardness from glass-fronted boxes. However, standing on the embankment itself, the view to each side along the river is more impressive. To the west stands Battersea Bridge, whose lines, and the spectacular sunsets beyond, inspired paintings by J.M.W. Turner (1775-1851) and James Whistler (1834-1903), both of whom at one time lived in houses facing the river. The sunsets are still a feature of the view, but the original bridge was diagnosed as suffering from 'a slight curvature to the west' and so was demolished in 1885 in favour of the present sturdier, more functional structure, which, even though tastefully painted in duck-egg blue and russet, cannot

The parade is led by the band of the Grenadier Guards (left), behind whom come veteran cyclists (top left), drum majorettes (top right and above), carnival queens and their princesses (centre left) and youthful brass bands (centre right). However, for some the excitement is all just too much (facing page).

Far left: spectators rest in the shadow of Battersea Power Station, whilst participants lean on their cycles, whether veteran (left) or trick (below). Horsedrawn omnibuses of the 1850s, the Fulham Firestars Juvenile Jazz Band, and a Mexican-style float from the West Country all add to the colour and vitality of the parade.

match the romantic aspect of the old.

Immediately downriver rise the fairy-tale pinnacles and pink and white tracery of Albert Bridge, built in 1873. At either end of this is posted an ominous warning: 'All troops must break step when marching over the bridge'. Whatever incident inspired this notice must have occurred some time ago — certainly the notice has been displayed ever since my own childhood. Further downriver are the four flat arches of Chelsea Bridge, which was built in 1937 and marks the far end of Battersea Park on the south bank. Above the park looms Battersea Power Station, monstrous symbol of modernity, looking for all the world like a massive, upturned billiard table.

It is said that both Julius Caesar and the Emperor Claudius crossed the river at about this point in their separate attempts to subjugate the Britons. The area on the south bank was known as Patricesy in the time of William the Conqueror, but was already known as Battersea when Henry St John (1678-1751), Lord Bolingbroke was born there, later taking it as his seat.

Bolingbroke was a brilliant, if erratic, politician and writer whose wife was a niece of Louis XIV's mistress, Madame de Maintenon. His links with the borough are commemorated in two local street names, Bolingbroke Walk and Bolingbroke Grove.

For many years Battersea was more renowned for its asparagus beds than for urban development, and a map dating from 1834 shows the area as a stretch of largely open country, of which the part bordering on the river was called Battersea Fields. Not that any nineteenth-century conservationist could claim that the countryside would be ruined by development, as

Sir Walter Besant (1836-1901), critic, novelist, and historian, confirmed: 'I myself remember the old Battersea Fields perfectly well; one shivers at the recollection; they were low, flat, damp, and, I believe, treeless; they were crossed, like Hackney Marsh, by paths raised above the level; at no time of the year could the Battersea Fields look anything but dreary. In winter they were inexpressibly dismal.' This is how they must have looked on the occasion in 1829 of an extraordinary duel, one of whose protagonists was no less a personage than the prime minister of the day, Arthur Wellesley (1769-1852), Duke of Wellington.

Top: pearly princes and princesses carry on the traditions of the pearlies. Above left: trumpeter, why are you bashful now? The drums of the Grenadier Guards carry the names (above) of all the campaigns in which the regiment has fought since the band was formed in 1656.

What sparked off this unlikely event was the Duke's support of the Catholic Emancipation Act, which aimed to remove the restrictions imposed upon Catholics. One of the Duke of Wellington's most zealous and vociferous opponents was George William Finch-Hatton (1791-1858), ninth Earl of Winchelsea, who was unwise enough to write a letter to the press accusing the Duke of 'insidious designs'. The Duke, as anxious to court public sympathy as to obtain redress, demanded an apology which, exactly as he anticipated, was not forthcoming. He challenged Winchelsea to a duel in Battersea Fields, where he rode one misty March morning with his second. A doctor, fetched out of bed by a peremptory message, was already there, his eyes opening ever wider with astonishment when he recognised the identity of one prospective patient. The Winchelsea contingent arrived late. The seconds conferred for the last time and handed out the pistols. The Duke had been wondering all morning whether to kill his man. If he did, he might have to await trial

in prison, which would be inconvenient for a prime minister. A voice cried, 'Fire!' The sixty-year-old Duke, Field Marshal, Commander in Chief of the Army and victor at Waterloo, fired ... and missed. Winchelsea then fired into the air, whereupon his second flourished a sheet of paper, from which he read aloud a withdrawal of Winchelsea's offensive remark. The Duke listened. 'But this is no apology,' he observed tartly. After a moment of hesitation, the magic word was written in. The Duke bowed frostily to his opponent, touched his hat, and rode away.

In 1858, two hundred acres of Battersea Fields were transformed into Battersea Park, doubtless providing some consolation for the habitués of the famous Vauxhall Gardens further downstream when these were closed in 1859. Following this, in 1860, came the founding of the Battersea Dogs Home, which still does sterling work sheltering stray cats and dogs. At the turn of the century, Battersea was a largely working-class area, but the park itself was in great demand from another section of the London public. Richard Church (1893-1972), poet and

novelist, who was born in the borough, has described their revolutionary activities: 'When I was a child, at the period when the bicycle was a novelty, High Society from over the River used the circular road in Battersea Park as a track. Grooms wheeled the bicycles to the Park, to await the arrival of the ladies and gentlemen in their carriages. The bicycles were mounted, with the aid of grooms, and for an hour or more the toffs (as the aristocracy was called in those days) pedalled round and round the Park, enraptured by this new form of constitutional exercise. Then, after the cyclists dismounted, the carriages disappeared, the nobility drove away, and the grooms wheeled the bicycles out of the Park.'

The parade is a multi-cultural occasion, embracing the eccentricity of the English (above), the flamboyance of the Caribbean (above left) and the peaceful philosophy of the Hare Krishnas (far left) from the Indian Cultural Centre in Croydon. Volunteers from Rotary International (centre left) work hard to maximise the benefits of the parade for charity. Left: the Mayor of Wandsworth, whose Council organised the parade, with the Harlow Crystals Show Corps. Top left: running repairs.

The original Pearly Kings and Queens Association was established in 1875 and its members (left and facing page) are energetic and colourful collectors for charity. Below: Oriental magic provides the theme of a float from Somerset.

In 1951 the tradition of Battersea Park as the leafy haunt of lovers and the site of discreet picnics, of family perambulations and of pursuits no noisier than boating on the lakes, tennis on the municipal courts and cricket on the broad swathes of grass, was broken in a way which caused nearby residents some alarm. A funfair was opened to celebrate the Festival of Britain, and it has been operating cheerfully ever since. Given the good-natured crowds and the joyful noises that were generated by the funfair, it was perhaps a natural, though imaginative, development to choose Battersea Park as the venue for an annual Easter Parade. This riot of colour, music and well-regulated movement benefits national and international charities and includes numerous exciting events, activities and spectacles, of which the parade itself is only one. The whole occasion, indeed, is one vast charitable exercise whose twin themes of enjoyment and involvement for spectators and participants alike reflect both the Christian celebration of Easter and the pagan festival of the goddess Eostre from which its name derives.

The Veteran Cycle Club (top left) rides in the parade to recall the early history of Battersea Park as an upper class cycle track. Things may be less glamorous behind the scenes (above far left), but the parade is an occasion for dressing up, whether officially (above left) or for fun (above).

Spring
'THE CLUB' – EASTER MONDAY

In the seventeenth century, a philanthropic movement began to establish and maintain friendly societies. These were voluntary associations which helped their members in sickness, old age and poverty, and which had links with some of the activities of the medieval guilds. The first general Act of Parliament concerning friendly societies was not passed until 1793, although a measure had been passed as early as 1757 compelling coalheavers working on the River Thames to contribute to a friendly society supervised by an alderman of the City of London. Further acts followed, the most comprehensive being that of 1875. The purposes of such societies were designated as including the relief

There was a Royal Navy dockyard at Sheerness from 1665, when Samuel Pepys supervised its construction, to 1960 and the working men's club (these pages) has survived its closure. Easter Monday at the club is a great family occasion, bringing together both sexes and all generations within the walls of that essentially male bastion.

or support of members and their families in sickness, other infirmity, or old age; the payment of burial expenses; insurance on the birth of their children; relief in the event of unemployment, shipwreck, or other distress; and insurance of a member's tools of trade. Working men's clubs were also set up 'to promote social intercourse, mental and moral improvement, and recreation'. Female friendly societies had existed since at least the 1790s, mainly to provide for the 'lying-in month' of married working women. As late as 1875 female friendly societies were in the habit of holding meetings in public houses, and it was customary to allocate a specific portion of

the society's funds to be spent on liquor at such functions. A Royal Commission frowned on this tradition, concluding, 'If the absolute prohibition of any sort of club is defensible, that of women's clubs meeting in public houses has most to be said for it.' Later, the tendency of some working men's clubs, as of some upper-class clubs, to degenerate into mere drinking and, sometimes, gambling dens, led to all clubs being included in the Licensing Act of 1902. Today, with the Welfare State undertaking many of the social, medical and educational functions of the friendly society, the working men's club still exists for the provision of 'social intercourse and recreation'.

The Easter bonnet parade (this page) is properly an American tradition. However, it provides an opportunity for parents and children alike to exercise their imagination and ingenuity as would-be milliners. The results range from the conventionally pretty to the purely fantastic and are as great a source of delight to the audience as to their wearers.

Spring
SPRINGTIME IN LONDON

Springtime in London begins in St James's Park, that irregular but cunningly designed area of green longitudinally bisected by a lake on which exotic ducks, geese and the occasional indigenous pelican have been cavorting with varying degrees of dignity since the seventeenth century. During the winter months, St James's Park is almost exclusively the

haunt of civil servants on their way to and from work, marching briskly through in the morning and surging back at night. Those who cross the park on their way between Green Park tube station in Piccadilly and their offices in Whitehall follow the route, did they but know it, that Charles I traced, with every air of bravery, on his way to the scaffold in 1649. But their insouciance may be forgiven in light of the fact that Charles II himself, instead of regarding the park as a shrine to his father, made it his favourite spot for

relaxation and also, no doubt, for dalliance. In springtime these same civil servants come out into the park at lunchtime with their packets of sandwiches and their flasks of tea or coffee to ward off the lingering cold of winter. As the days become warmer, some may even take the opportunity to follow the example of that most industrious of civil servants, Samuel Pepys, who, one day in 1666, 'lay down upon the grass and slept awhile'. The region of London to which St James's Park belongs is, in effect, one vast

Horse Guards Parade acts like a magnet on some visitors (top left), whilst others prefer the parks for watching the world go by (top right) or the grass grow (centre). In spring, St James's Park fills with congregations of visitors (above left) and flowers (above).

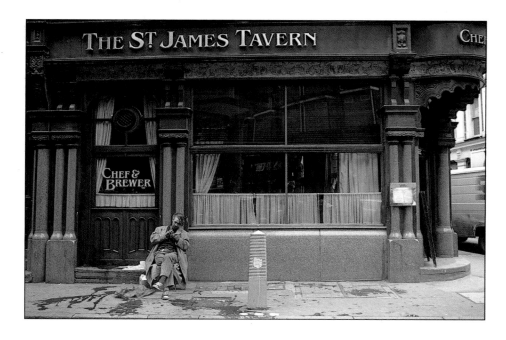

savanna, which also includes Green Park, Hyde Park, Kensington Gardens and the hidden gardens of Buckingham Palace. In the early morning and evening, and at lunch time, movement in St James's Park is particularly brisk, having about it an air of informal orchestration. At other times there is less urgency, as prams, with their occupants and handlers, pensioners and tourists annex the paths and the grassy bumps and hollows. Not only is St James's Park historic in itself, but history is continually being made all around it. At the opposite end to Buckingham Palace, between the park's eastern extremity and Whitehall, lie the Admiralty, the Treasury and the Foreign Office. Here too is Downing Street, where the official residences of the prime minister and the chancellor of the exchequer are situated. A proverbial stone's throw away lie the

In contrast to the springtime idyll of the daffodils in St James's Park (above), the streets of London offer a different perspective. For some (top) the streets are home, and the only time to call this home your own is early in the morning before the crowds are up and milling. For others (above left), the streets are an impromptu portrait studio and a guardsman is an essential prop. For others again (below left), the streets are the place for indulging in that favourite London pastime, waiting for a bus.

Houses of Parliament and Westminster Abbey. For tourists in particular there is a further attraction. Fronting onto Whitehall, and separated from St James's Park by Horse Guards Parade, is Horse Guards itself and, incongruous amid the bustle and fumes of a major city thoroughfare, a guard of real horses. Their function, and that of the sentries who ride them, swords drawn, is purely ceremonial. The troopers themselves belong to the Household Cavalry, whose original duty was to protect the sovereign and the royal family, as well as the metropolis itself. The red tunics and white plumes belong to the Life Guards, formed in 1660 on the Restoration of the Monarchy as the personal bodyguard of Charles II. The blue tunics and red plumes belong to the Blues and Royals, a composite regiment formed from the Royal Horse Guards and the 1st Dragoons. Patience and an impassive nature are the most important qualities required by both sentries and their mounts. These days, provocation comes not from potential regicides, but from eager amateur photographers, and even more eager tourists, determined to get into the picture.

'London, thou art the flower of cities all,' expostulated the poet William Dunbar at the beginning of the sixteenth century. This was really quite a compliment coming from a Scot. Some 350 years later, however, Benjamin Disraeli, who was the first British political novelist as well as the premier British politician of his time, wrote that 'London is a modern Babylon'. Springtime in London highlights both these characteristics. In particular, it heralds a sharp increase in the babble of tongues, as the chatter of tourists mingles with the many different dialects, accents and languages spoken by London's permanent residents.

Whitening and polishing are still the lot of the guardsman (facing page), if he is to maintain that immaculate appearance which the public expects (far left). London buses (left) are jocularly said to hunt in packs of three or more, with long waits inbetween. Below: building and repair work has to be fitted in around the rest of London's busy life.

Far left: arriving and waiting at a London rail terminal. Above: the sentry's eye view, or how the guardsman sees the tourists as they pass Horse Guards on their sightseeing bus. Left: the dusty interior and reverential atmosphere of the British Museum in Bloomsbury, where noise and sunlight are equally discouraged in the interests of the public's concentration and the preservation of the exhibits.

Spring
THE BOAT RACE

The boat race, as it has now been known for 160 years, is on the face of it an unlikely candidate for national fervour and profound partisanship. Instituted in 1829, it was, and still is, a supposedly private contest between the universities of Oxford and Cambridge. It is initiated afresh each year by the previous year's losers, who issue a personal challenge to the winners. The race is between two rowing boats, each propelled by eight brawny students whose average weight is between thirteen and fourteen stone. The Oxford crew of 1988 were the heaviest on record weighing over three-quarters of a ton. The crews cover the course between Putney and Mortlake on the River Thames at about the pace of a marathon runner, starting at the exact moment that the tide

turns. As none of the oarsmen can see where they are going, they are dependent on the direction of their cox, a fellow student, male or female, who sits at the back of the boat shouting orders and manipulating the rudder-lines. The race is usually decided in the first mile and a quarter, after which the boat that is in front is able to take the most favourable course, leaving the trailing crew no choice but to fall in behind and become the back end of a procession of two. Sometimes the proceedings are enlivened by one of the oarsmen missing his stroke. This is called 'catching a crab' and is painful for the perpetrator and potentially disastrous for his crew. Only twice in the forty-four races since World War II has the distance between the two crews at the finish been as little as a 'canvas', as the boat's tapered front end is called. There are few rules. Barging your opponent out of the way is illegal, but intimidation is tolerated. If one of the boats sinks before the end of the first half mile, calculated as the length of the Fulham Wall, the race is re-rowed on another day. This happened in 1951 when Oxford sank and then lost the replay by one of the biggest margins on record.

In 1984, Cambridge achieved the unique feat of

Early morning is a good time for rowers to adjust their oars (top left) and for spectators to choose a prime position (top right). From its canvas (above left) to its hull (centre), the Oxford boat is the very best that modern boatbuilding can provide – as is, of course, its Cambridge counterpart. Partisanship is evident everywhere (above and left), although the sponsor stays neutral and opts for glamour instead (facing page).

sinking before the start, when their cox, momentarily blinded by the bulk of the oarsmen in front of him, steered into a defenceless barge, hitting it head on and damaging his own boat irrevocably. This race was also re-rowed on another day, when Cambridge, in a substitute boat, lost. Of course, if a boat sinks beyond the symbolic safety of the Fulham Wall, then it's just bad luck. This happened to Cambridge in 1978, and to Oxford in 1925. In 1912, both crews sank.

The race is followed on U.K. television by over ten million people, which makes it the third most popular televised sporting event after the Football Association Cup Final and the Grand National. An estimated 150 million people watch it worldwide. To these must be added the many thousands who crowd the towpaths lining the course and the bridges and buildings overlooking it. Only a tiny proportion of this vast audience has any interest in rowing as a sport or any connection with either university, yet they all display loyalty to one side or the other, and favours of the appropriate light or dark blue find a ready market.

Left: programme sellers, diplomatically wearing mid-blue. Below: after achieving victory by five and a half lengths, the 1988 Oxford crew are helped ashore by their boatmen.

This has always been the case. The first race, rowed at Henley, was such a success that the event was moved permanently to London. Since 1864 it has been rowed from Putney to Mortlake. An eyewitness wrote of the 1870 race: 'Every man shook out his finest suit: every woman drew forth her dress, that to her mind, best became her. Nay the poorest got their mites of finery. The lucifer-boys habited in rags of surprising and complicated tenacity, sported their bit of deep or pale blue .... But the holiday was for all London: for Parliament and people, for the Heir Apparent in the Umpire's boat, and for the workfolk lining the sylvan shores .... They who had blue dresses

were indeed fortunate, and sported them: they who could afford to buy, bought, and were happy. Every London apprentice aired one University colour. I verily believe that the drunkard was on that day happy as he stroked his blue nose.'

For the supremely fit crews, the race itself is the culmination of many months of agonising trials and exhausting training. All this has to be fitted in around the student's normal graduate or post-graduate work, for the true amateur spirit survives in these young men. Strength, power, and even technique, are not enough on their own. The balance of the crew, the position of each man in it, and even the side of the

Centre left: the reserve crews from Cambridge and Oxford, called Goldie and Isis respectively, prepare to race over the same course as a curtain-raiser to the big race. Above left: supporters with mixed allegiances are nevertheless all smiles, as are the sponsor's representatives (above).

Far left: Mike Gaffney, the Oxford stroke, comes ashore, jubilation mixed with relief. Left: an old Oxford blue wears his rowing cap above more spiritual garb. Below: spectators in the Isis boathouse watch the finish.

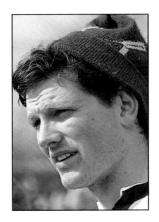

Left: Denis Thatcher, husband of Britain's Prime Minister, presents the sponsor's trophy to Christopher Penny, the Oxford President, as Mike Gaffney (above) looks on.

boat on which he rows are paramount. Traditionally, being awarded a rowing blue, the only reward for participating in the boat race, is a greater honour than any other blue. This seems only fair when one considers the long-drawn-out trauma of the months leading up to the race, and the physical and mental anguish of the race itself. In 1980, Oxford won by the proverbial canvas after their bowman, an eighteen-year-old straight from school, collapsed with a third of the course still to row. Utmost drama dogged the preliminaries to the 1987 race. In 1986, after ten straight Oxford victories, Cambridge finished streets ahead. The following year Oxford mustered a

formidable nucleus of American international oarsmen. After a long-running altercation, the entire American contingent walked out, leaving Oxford just six weeks in which to find, and train up, a new crew. In the words of their coach, Daniel Topolski, 'It was not the worst crew I had ever coached, but this year Cambridge had a top-class eight, and most of our crew did not believe for one moment that we could win.' But win they did, by four lengths, under the inspiration of their President, Donald Macdonald, a 29-year-old mature student who had slogged his way to university by taking evening classes, whilst supporting his wife and three children as a full-time insurance salesman.

Spring
INTERNATIONAL CLOWNS' CONVENTION

In Shakespeare's *Hamlet* (2,2), the Prince of Denmark says 'The Clown shall make those laugh whose lungs are tickle o' the sere', i.e. ready to burst out laughing. The international clowns who descend each year on the seaside resort of Bognor Regis to meet and make merry amongst the residents and other visitors are part of an English tradition which goes back even further than Shakespeare, and which has absorbed elements from other cultures along the way. Contrary to appearances, being a professional clown is a serious business, with its own distinctive range of costumes, make-up, routines and terminology. Properly speaking, clowns are the elegant performers with white faces who wear conical hats and spangled costumes decorated with pom-poms. The tramp-like stooges who shamble around spoiling the clowns' acts or serve as the butt of it all, are augusts, so called after the French low comedy star of the 1860s called Auguste. It is the august who is on the receiving end of all those buckets of whitewash, custard pies and cakes lavishly smothered with cream. The cream is actually shaving soap and the secret, when you get a cake in the face, is to shut your eyes and blow out through your mouth, so as not to swallow any of the 'cream'.

The earliest clowns were comic actors in the Greek and Roman theatre who were outside the action of the play and established a rapport with the audience by

parodying the other characters' movements and sometimes pelting the spectators with nuts.

Clowning was an inherent part of the entertainment provided by the itinerant minstrels and jugglers in the Middle Ages. However, the first proper clown to appear on the English stage grew out of a character in the mystery plays called Old Vice. His function was to play tricks on the serious characters, especially the Devil, and to indulge in general horseplay. By the time of Shakespeare, three distinct types of stage clown could be distinguished: the simpleton, such as Costard in *Love's Labour's Lost;* the out-and-out knave, such as Autolycus in *A Winter's Tale;* and the court jester, such as Touchstone in *As You Like It.* The most

Left: pupils of South Bersted Church of England Primary School enjoy watching the clowns, whilst being clowns themselves for the day. Facing page bottom left: clowns take their business very seriously. A clown's make-up is traditional, yet each variation is unique to its owner and is always precisely applied. Not a policeman at all, Bluey the Clown (facing page top left) is one of the organisers of the convention.

famous Elizabethan clowns were Richard Tarleton (died 1588), supposedly the original Yorick, the dead jester referred to in *Hamlet;* his pupil Robert Armin (c.1568-c.1611); and William Kempe (died 1603). Kempe even took a touring company of English comics to Denmark and Germany. Thus, an English actor found his way into the comic tradition of Germany. He was Robert Reynolds (died c.1650), who appeared in Germany as Pickelhering, a character who has survived to this day, his trappings of ill-fitting clothes and shoes little changed. In exchange, as it were, for Pickelhering, Europe gave Britain two of the elements from which the modern clown has evolved: the Italian commedia dell'arte, in which the characters

made up their speeches as they went along and the broader humour was supplied by comic servants, and the harlequinade, its French derivation.

One of the stock characters in the commedia dell'arte was Arlecchino, a quick-witted, knavish servant. In the English harlequinades of the early eighteenth century, Arlecchino had been transformed, via the French tradition, into Harlequin, appearing first as a romantic magician and then as a star-crossed lover. Into the act came Pierrot, a simpleton with a bald head and flour-whitened face, who wore a loose white tunic with long sleeves, and who, under the French influence, had developed that strain of melancholy which is one of the traditional

characteristics of the modern clown.

The original circus clown, though he never appeared in the circus ring, was Joseph Grimaldi (1778-1837). His father, the Italian-born ballet master at Drury Lane Theatre, was a man with a sense of humour. During the anti-Catholic riots of 1780 in London, he rubbed out the slogan 'No Popery', which had been scribbled on his door, and substituted 'No religion'. Grimaldi's mother, Rebecca Brooker, was a dancer and a versatile actress.

'Joe' Grimaldi first appeared on the stage at the age of three, as an infant dancer in a pantomime at Sadler's Wells Theatre. Either that same year or the next, he also performed at Drury Lane. The boy came to be in such demand that, soon after his father's death in 1788, he was booked to appear in pantomimes simultaneously at Drury Lane and Sadler's Wells, which he did by running between the two. His hobbies at that time were breeding pigeons and collecting insects, of which he is said to have had four

thousand specimens. In a role specially written for him in a Christmas show at Covent Garden Theatre in 1806, *Harlequin and Mother Goose: or, The Golden Egg*, he turned Pierrot into a star part. The simpleton became Joey, the clown, and clowns are called 'Joey' to this day. The love scenes between Harlequin and Columbine in the original plays eventually became little more than intermittent pas de deux interposed between bouts of outrageous horseplay such as have become the stock in trade of the modern circus clown. These include slippery slides for the unsuspecting, pails of whitewash, hot pokers applied to the seats of trousers, mock battles with fruit and other household missiles, conjuring tricks, and acrobatics. Joe's athletic and exhausting routines ruined his health, and he retired in 1823. His place was taken by his son, whose dissolute habits contributed to his death in 1832 at the age of thirty. Grimaldi made a final stage appearance on 27 June 1828, when he played Harlequin from a wheelchair.

The outstanding clown of this century was Grock (1880-1959), whose real name was Adrien Wettach. Grock was actually born in Switzerland, but played in

London almost continuously from 1911 to 1924, mainly at the Coliseum Theatre. Grock was a white-face clown whose act was performed entirely in mime, though in such a way that every nuance and joke was immediately understood by the audience, from whom he extracted the utmost sympathy with his melancholy aspect and visibly human failings.

These pages: which are the real clowns? Sometimes it's difficult to tell as Bognor's residents and visitors take advantage of this annual opportunity to assume another persona and join the zany world of the clown for a while.

Far left: Arturo, a traditional white-faced clown. Left: beware, clowns crossing! Below and facing page: a convention-al christening! Bongo, alias Trevor Pharo, and his wife, Angela, chose this jolly occasion for the christening of their son, Ryan Harvey. The vicar, the Reverend Pruen, also conducted a Sunday Clowns' Service in Bognor's Royal Hall.

The professional clown is a consummate artist. The International Clowns' Convention confirms not only the artistry of the modern clown, but also his professionalism and his dedication to his craft. During the convention there are lectures, seminars and workshops on historical mime, juggling, make-up, balloonistics and marketing your act. Clowns flock to Bognor from many parts of the world. There is Fulvio from Switzerland, Olli from Germany, Ruben and Raimondo from Sweden and Rainbow T. from the USA. From the UK come Jojo and Bobo, Charlie and Lee, Barney, Kerby Drill, Bluey, Zippo, Bingo, the dual performer, mime-Auguste and white-face clown, Arthur Vercoe Pedlar, and a host of others. The event is not just for the clowns and their families. The Clowns' Convention bus tours local schools, hospitals, community centres and old people's homes, spreading the message. One entire primary school, teachers as well as pupils, has abandoned the traditional classroom approach to the topic of 'Clowns' in favour of becoming clowns themselves for the day. Holiday-makers and residents, policemen and traffic wardens all join in. 'Welcome to Clownsville' proclaims a notice outside the town. Several hundred yards farther on, a policewoman is directing the traffic. There is nothing odd in this, except that she is wearing a clown's red nose. What the townsfolk really think about these annual goings-on is unknown. However, there is a sneaking suspicion that the sentiments of the fifteenth-century vicar who wrote to his Prior, begging 'that I may cease to work at Bognor' would find little sympathy amongst his twentieth-century counterparts.

Spring

CAMMEL LAIRD SHIPYARD, BIRKENHEAD

Britons have been building ships since the Stone Age. The earliest of these were sturdy enough both to have brought farmers and their families to Britain from continental Europe, and to have carried a whole community of them onwards to Orkney more than four thousand years ago. After the Bronze Age, the Celts arrived in Britain. Their ships traded in copper with Ireland, and in gold and crafted goods between parts of Britain and with the continent. The ships also brought tin, one ingredient of bronze, from Cornwall to the northwestern Highlands. In the fifth century A.D., an Irish fleet joined up with the Picts and the Saxons in a remarkable alliance which finally cleared Britain of the Romans, and Irish ships brought the people of Dal Riata, the Scots, to Argyll in about 500. Alfred the Great built galleys with forty to sixty oars on each side which proved larger and more powerful than those of the marauding Vikings. In the *Anglo-Saxon Chronicle*, Edgar, King of the English, is noted for his 'fleet so proud'. In 1190, Richard I, Coeur de Lion, sent nine large sailing vessels, 150 smaller ships, and thirty-eight galleys to the Holy Land.

Henry VII built the first proper naval ship. This was

Top left: the dry dock at Cammell Laird, Birkenhead, and (top right) work in the construction hall, whose huge dimensions, 145 metres long, 107 metres wide and 50 metres high, enable entire ships to be built within its walls. The work requires great concentration (above centre and left), so rest periods (centre left) and workplace camaraderie (above) are essential to maintain standards.

the *Henry Grace à Dieu*, equipped with 120 guns, including four sixty-pounders. Henry VIII made the Navy a distinct armed service, set up the Navy Board, and established dockyards at Deptford, Erith, Greenwich, and Woolwich. In 1512, James IV of Scotland had the *Great Michael* built, which one sixteenth-century historian claimed was 'the greatest ship and most of strength that *ever* sailed in England or France'. Chatham Dockyard was founded during the reign of Edward VI. Sir John Hawkyns (1532-95), Treasurer of the Navy Board, established a rebuilding programme, and it was his fleet that outmanoeuvred the Spanish Armada in 1588. Phineas Pett (1570-1647), first President of the Shipwrights' Company, designed Charles I's magnificent *Sovereign of the Seas*, the first British three-decker battleship. James II had twenty battleships rebuilt and sixty-nine others

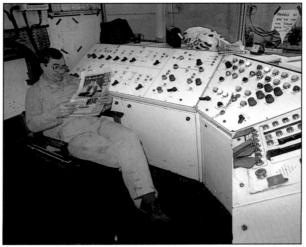

The original company was founded by William Laird, whose son, John Laird (1805-74), was a notable pioneer of shipbuilding. In 1861, John also became Birkenhead's first Member of Parliament. In 1903 Laird Brothers, as it was then known, joined with Charles Cammell and Co., the Sheffield steel manufacturers, to become Cammell Laird and Co. During World War I the company built thirty-three warships, including eight submarines, and duing World War II it built 106 fighting ships. The present-day company (this page) builds Royal Navy ships and submarines, tankers, oil rig units, and sea-going helicopter bases.

repaired. The Industrial Revolution not only transformed both the materials from which ships were made and their means of propulsion, but also relocated the shipbuilding industry to areas, such as Clydeside and Tyneside, where there were readily available supplies of coal and iron ore. By 1914, the Clyde shipyards were building about half the world's tonnage. However, the depression of the 1930s halted operations on the Clyde and brought such hardship to Tyneside that thousands joined a hunger march from Jarrow to London. Today the Clyde and Tyneside shipyards offer only shadowy reminders of their former glories. Nevertheless, the Birkenhead Iron Works, founded on the Mersey in 1824 by a Clydesider, still prospers, as Cammell Laird Shipbuilders.

Whether working by night in one of the dry docks (above centre) or by day on a new hull (above), the break at the control panel (top) or the pause for coffee with pin-ups (left), are an important part of the shift for today's shipbuilder (above left).

Spring

LAKELAND – A VIEW OF SPRING

The Lake District is now embraced administratively under the ancient name of Cumbria, which comes from the Welsh *Cymry*, meaning 'the brethren'. This is what the oppressed Celtic tribes in the west of Britain called themselves in the Dark Ages after the Romans had left, and so present-day Cumbria recalls the fact that many of them found refuge and survived in the mountains of Lakeland. This stupendous mélange of rocky fells, soft woodlands, and breathtaking expanses of green contains within its 700 acres all the principal English lakes and the largest national park in Britain. There are traces of rare volcanic ash, or tuff, on the summit of Pike O'Stickle, whilst tiny pockets of woodland contain vestiges of the natural forest which once entirely covered Britain, but which had been largely destroyed by man even before the end of the prehistoric period.

Towards the end of the eighteenth century, the awesome nature of the countryside, as well as its beauty, had begun to attract tourists to the area. They came in their carriages, bringing hordes of servants to cater for their needs. They revelled particularly in the

Green swards (top left) quickly give way to more rugged skylines. Whether viewed from a road near Buttermere (top right), or from across the River Derwent at Grange Bridge (centre), or from beneath a lowering sky (left), the mountains of the Lake District are never less than awe-inspiring. The calm of the lakes themselves, such as Ullswater (above) punctuates the drama of the mountains.

soaring peaks, in the dramatic cloudscapes, in the weird mists that rose from the surfaces of the lakes, and in the echoes that reverberated all around. Should the natural echoes not suffice, there was a barge on Ullswater, equipped with a small cannon, which, for a consideration, would provide an artificial one: 'To an echo, first quality, 10/-; To ditto, second quality, 5/-'. These tourists also came to experience the fearful excitement and vision of solitude that had drawn artists and poets to the area. The latter had discovered in the district an environment reflecting the fashionable ideas of the Swiss philosopher, Jean Jacques Rousseau. Here was a place where the noble savage lurking inside the man of taste could manifest itself, where the well-bred lady could feel herself to be a child of nature, and where the landscape could inspire both with beautiful and creative thoughts during the course of an evening stroll. A market-

Far left: a farmhouse at Dockray, by Ullswater, whitewashed in the traditional local manner. Left: taking a break on the shores of Buttermere. Wordsworth took a break here with his sister in 1804, leaving his wife and three-week-old daughter at home in Grasmere. He hoped to rekindle his poetic inspiration. Twelve years later he came again, with his wife's sister, Sara Hutchinson, to advise a friend on planting his estate with native trees. The poet's advice on matters of conservation was much sought after and often heeded.

orientated artist, Thomas Smith of Derby, started the Lake District vogue in 1761, publishing a series of his own engravings of the region. These inspired a positive invasion of painters, including Poussin, Gainsborough, and Turner, all of whom recorded their impressions on canvas. The poet Gray, author of the most popular poem of the day, *Elegy Written in a Country Churchyard*, came equipped with a notebook and Claude-glass, an ingenious device that, it was claimed, enhanced appreciation of the view. In 1799, Gray was followed by two young men who settled in the region and took it as their inspiration for a new kind of poetry. They were William Wordsworth and Samuel Taylor Coleridge, originators of the Romantic Movement. Early November 1799, found them striding west from Keswick to Lorton, then taking the road to the south. Coleridge, an opium addict, established an extended household at Greta Hall, near Keswick, where, after a few years, he left his wife and children to the care of another Lakes poet, Robert Southey. He himself stayed with Wordsworth, before going to London, where, for eighteen years until his death, he lodged with the doctor in whose care he had originally placed himself for a month. Dove Cottage, in Grasmere, where Wordsworth lived with both his wife, Mary, and his sister, Dorothy, has been preserved almost exactly as it was in their time. Visitors still come to the Lake District to walk, climb and revel in the views and the solitude, just as the first tourists did two hundred years ago. Lakeland continues to exert its magic and creative power.

Above left: a Lake District time trial, a true test of a cyclist's mental and physical stamina. Above: traditional slate boundary walls reflect the geological composition, as well as the starkness, of the peaks beyond.

Spring

Royal Salute, Hyde Park

Hyde Park is an enormous expanse of green to be found in such a central position in a capital city and it has survived the jealous stares of speculators only because it belongs to the sovereign and is maintained by the Crown. This has not always been the case. Originally, it was part of the Manor of Hyde, which belonged to Westminster Abbey. It was when Henry VIII dissolved the monasteries in 1536, that he appropriated the land and stocked it as a deer forest, where he gave private hunting parties for his cronies.

The salute for HM the Queen's birthday on 21 April is fired by the King's Troop of the Royal Horse Artillery from field guns of a similar pattern to those used at the Battle of Waterloo. The Queen has another, official, birthday in June, which, usually means better weather for the public and other celebrants. Chelsea Pensioners (left) are amongst London's more colourful denizens, dressed in their scarlet tunics and black caps, which were adapted from uniforms worn at the time of the Duke of Marlborough's campaigns in the early eighteenth century.

James I opened the park to the public and Charles I built the Ring, a circular carriageway about 250 yards in diameter, around which the fashionable would ride or drive and generally show off. After the execution of Charles I, Parliament sold the park for development, but not before Puritan objections had been raised against the 'most shameful powder'd-hair men, and painted and spotted women' who frequented it. Fortunately the developers were slow to take advantage of their purchase, so, when Charles II was restored to the throne, Hyde Park was restored to the public, and the Ring to the exhibitionists. It was here that Samuel Pepys' (1633-1703) horse ran away with him, so that he failed to catch the eye of either the King or the

King's mistress, Lady Castlemaine (1640-1709). The dramatist William Wycherley (1640-1716) was luckier. Not only did he catch the eye of the lady, now elevated to Duchess of Cleveland, but she addressed a comment to him about his first play. This was the beginning of a close relationship between them. The function of the Ring was later assumed by the Ride, where, in Victorian times, rode 'only the gently born and gently nurtured, driving the heat and faintness of the ballroom out, by spirited canters through a grove of such leaves as only our well-abused English climate can produce'.

The park's deer proliferated until the beginning of the eighteenth century, when they were replaced by muggers and footpads. Retribution for those who were caught came in the form of flogging, hanging, or both, at Tyburn, the northeast corner of the park,

where Marble Arch now stands. The only public spectacle there these days is Speaker's Corner, whose orators are unmolested except by hecklers. Hyde Park was also at one time a favourite duelling ground, particularly in the eighteenth century. The curiously-shaped Serpentine lake was built in 1730 at the instigation of Queen Caroline. It became very popular with would-be suicides, some of whom sadly succeeded, in spite of the resuscitation equipment available. One such unfortunate was Harriet, the unhappy first wife of the poet Shelley, who drowned herself in 1816. The park has continued to take its grisly toll. As recently as the 1970s, two overenthusiastic wedding guests drowned attempting to swim across the Serpentine fully clothed. In 1982, a remote-controlled IRA nail bomb of huge capacity killed and maimed soldiers, spectators, and horses, as a mounted troop

The uniform of the King's Troop of the Royal Horse Artillery dates from the early nineteenth century. The Latin motto translates as 'Everywhere, wherever right and glory lead'.

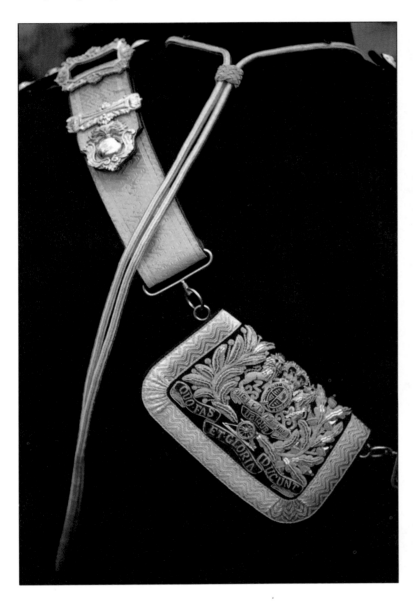

rode along the Carriage Road.

However, the sounds of artillery that emanate from Hyde Park several times a year are purely ceremonial. Hyde Park is one of London's two official Saluting Stations, the other being the wharf of the Tower of London, from which solemn salutes are traditionally fired on certain royal occasions. A sixty-two-gun salute is fired on the anniversaries of the birth, accession, and coronation of the sovereign, and on the birthdays of HM the Queen Mother and HRH the Duke of Edinburgh. On extraordinary and triumphal occasions, such as the opening of Parliament by the sovereign in person or the birth of a royal baby, a forty-one-gun salute is fired.

Chelsea Pensioners are old or invalided soldiers who live a privileged but still militarily orientated existence in the Royal Hospital, Chelsea. This elegant building was designed for Charles II by Sir Christopher Wren.

Spring

SHAKESPEARE'S BIRTHDAY

The Shakespeare phenomenon was slow to get off the ground. The Rev. John Ward, who was Vicar of Stratford-upon-Avon from 1662 to 1681, wrote in his notebook: 'Remember me to peruse Shakespeare's plays and be versed in them that I be not ignorant in that matter.' Here was the incumbent of the very church in which Shakespeare had been buried some fifty years earlier confessing that he really ought to have a look at the man's plays sometime. Today, about half a million people visit Shakespeare's birthplace every year. Once a year, on his supposed birthday, the town hosts a special celebration, including a procession from the Town Hall to the Church, where a service is held in his honour.

The actual date of Shakespeare's birth is unknown, but he was baptised in the Parish Church on 26 April 1564 and, as he died on 23 April 1616, that day has also been assumed, for reasons of convenience, to be his birthday. The next firm date we know of in Shakespeare's life is 28 November 1582, when he was eighteen. On that day a bond was issued for his

marriage to Anne Hathaway, eight years his senior. Their daughter Susanna was born less than six months later, for she was baptised on 26 May 1583. Twins followed in 1585. This is all we know for certain about Shakespeare's early life, until a spiteful reference to him in a pamphlet written in 1592, from which it is clear that he was now beginning to make his name in London as an actor and writer. In 1599 he became a partner in the new Globe Theatre, the company being named the King's Men on the accession of James I in 1603. In 1610 he retired to his Stratford residence of New Place, the foremost house in the town, which he had bought in 1597 for sixty pounds, and interested

himself in business and property deals. Between about 1587 and 1611, a period of not much more than twenty years, he wrote some of the greatest plays and poetry the world has ever seen.

Shakespeare's two early narrative poems, *Venus and Adonis* and *Lucrece*, were dedicated to the young Earl of Southampton. We know from a literary commonplace book published in 1598 that Shakespeare had been circulating 'his sugred sonnets among his private friends'. These were, however, not published until 1609, when they were brought out by an adventurous publisher without their author's permission. The book is mysteriously dedicated to a

Facing page: 'And on his grave-stone this insculpture' (Timon of Athens, 5, 4). The simple inscription is almost overwhelmed by the mass of flowers for the service of remembrance. The occasion is marked by celebrations solemn and not so solemn (this page), as befits the poet who was a master of comedy as well as of tragedy.

'Two lads that thought there was no more behind, / But such a day tomorrow as today, / And to be boy eternal.' (The Winter's Tale, 1, 2).

'Mr W.H.', whose identity has never been satisfactorily explained. Shakespeare's sonnets appear to be addressed to three people. The first person is the poet's favoured friend, a young man who is being urged to get married. The second is a rival poet who has falsely ingratiated himself with the youth. The third is the poet's mistress, the famous dark lady of the sonnets, who has also been having an affair with the poet's friend. The true identity of these people has been a matter for speculation ever since. They surely existed, for the intensity which burns through the sequence of poems firmly suggests they are autobiographical, and this would seem to be confirmed by the fact that the sequence was never reissued in Shakespeare's lifetime. As with any long series of

Midsummer Night's Dream, the tragedy Romeo and Juliet, and the drama that hovers inbetween, The Merchant of Venice. From 1596 to 1599 he wrote the history plays Richard II, the two parts of Henry IV, in which Falstaff appears, and Henry V. These were followed by the fantasies – Much Ado about Nothing, As You Like It, and Twelfth Night. In 1601, his erstwhile patron, the Earl of Southampton, was committed to the Tower of London for his part in the Earl of Essex's rebellion. This probably had a greater effect on Shakespeare's dramatic art than did the death of Elizabeth I and the accession of James I, in 1603. It is to this period that the 'dark comedies' All's Well that Ends Well, Troilus and Cressida, and Measure for Measure belong. An even darker

poems not specifically written for publication, the quality of these sonnets varies, but numbers 18, 87, 89, 97, 98, 116, 130, 144, and 146 are amongst the very finest of their kind.

Shakespeare himself cared little about the publication of his plays. What are known, from the format in which they were first printed, as the Quartos are thought to be largely pirated editions written down by an energetic member of the audience during performances. The first official Folio edition was not published until seven years after Shakespeare's death. Amongst his earlier plays are The Comedy of Errors and Richard III, followed by the lyrical comedy A

Above: 'Did you never see the picture of "we three"?' (Twelfth Night, 2, 2). The office of beadle is a survival from Shakespeare's days. Left: Shakespeare's reputed birthplace. His father, John, was a glover and a prominent citizen of the town who, in spite of his occasional lapses into debt, was formally granted a coat of arms in 1599.

'Your visitation shall receive such thanks, / As fits a king's remembrance' (Hamlet, 2, 2). Left: a youthful section of the congregation at the annual service in the poet's memory come bearing daffodils.

phase had begun in 1599 with *Julius Caesar*, which was followed in 1601 by *Hamlet*, regarded by many critics worldwide as Shakespeare's greatest and most enigmatic tragedy. From then on, in *Othello*, *Macbeth*, *King Lear*, *Timon of Athens*, *Coriolanus*, and *Antony and Cleopatra*, he poured out his messages of poetic pessimism, depicting each of the major vices in turn: jealousy, lust for power, vanity, ingratitude and cruelty, pride, and sexual lust. To his final period belong the fairytales, *The Winter's Tale* and *The*

Tempest, and some of his sweetest poetry. The last play, in which he most probably collaborated with John Fletcher, literally brought the house down. An errant cannon in *Henry VIII* demolished the Globe Theatre in 1613 on the play's third performance. The most remarkable thing about Shakespeare's plays is that, though they were written in haste, for repertory companies who could not expect a run of more than a few performances, they still work so marvellously well today.

Floral tributes are the order of the day and come in all shapes and sizes, from the simple posy being wheeled to the church (top left) to the gifts of local schoolgirls (above centre) and the wreaths of academics (above). Even spectators look out over a brightly coloured window box (above left).

Spring

SCOTLAND IN APRIL

Scotland in April is like most other places in Britain in March; almost everything is that much later. Although Edward Topham, journalist, playwright, dandy, and philanderer, who spent six months in Edinburgh in 1774/75, observed with a neat blend of tartness and enthusiasm: 'There is one circumstance here which certainly deserves notice, as it is a contradiction to all the rules which are laid down in regard to climates; I mean, the early maturity of their women. It is generally imagined that cold has the same degree of influence over the animal, as it has over the vegetable world; but in this country they are in direct opposition; for the

plants are very late, and the girls extremely forward.'

It has been remarked that one reason for the ready way in which the Scots have traditionally accepted people from other races and cultures into their midst is that they are too busy hating the English to bother themselves overmuch about anyone else. Certainly, some Englishmen have given cause for offence by making caustic fun at Scottish expense. Samuel Johnson even shocked his most devoted biographer and amanuensis, the Scot, James Boswell, with one after-dinner sally: 'Sir, I believe you have a great many noble wild prospects. But, Sir, I believe the noblest prospect that a Scotsman ever sees is the road which leads him to England.' The Rev. Sydney Smith, who was a noted political figure as well as a country parson, referred to Scotland as 'that knuckle-end of England – that land of Calvin, oat-cakes, and sulphur'. Scotland is, even to the Scots themselves, a mysterious country. The highland line, which divides the country diagonally rather than horizontally, is not a boundary at all, but simply an imperceptible geological fault. The grand scenery of the Highlands as a setting for fantastical history, clans, tartans, kilts, and all its other romantic trappings, was largely the invention of novelist and poet, Sir Walter Scott, whose enthusiastic outpourings topped the best seller lists and were

Rugged mountains, dramatic castles and the glittering waters of lochs are part of many people's dream of Scotland. Top right: Eilean Donan Castle, and (left) the Post Office at Achlyness. Less dreamlike is the weather, although the grey is a foil for the scarlet gowns of the University of St Andrews (above and above centre). Sheep farming predominates in this harsh environment and the farmer and his dog are rulers of the moorland.

greatly loved by Queen Victoria herself.

The truth is that what are designated as the Lowlands offer much the same kind of attractions as the Highlands, and the traditional, but largely imaginary conflict, between the two is as nothing compared with the quarrels and rivalries that afflict other communities and groups within this arbitrary division: Macdonalds against Campbells, Glasgow against Edinburgh, Celtic against Rangers, and almost everyone against the MacGregors. More Scots, including several Highland clans, fought against than fought for Bonnie Prince Charlie in his ill-managed attempt to wrest the crowns of England and Scotland from the Hanoverian king, George II. At the final, fatal battle of Culloden, there were even cases of brother fighting against brother. The Church of Scotland was split asunder in 1843, when 190 ministers swept out of the Church's annual General Assembly to form the Free Church of Scotland, and schisms, amalgamations, and takeovers have been happening ever since, with the result that today there are five distinct Churches within the Scottish Presbyterian movement. Perhaps the philosopher

and writer, Robert Louis Stevenson, got as near as anyone to explaining the curious nature of Scottish identity when he wrote: 'Scotland is indefinable: it has no unity except upon the map. Two languages, many dialects, innumerable forms of piety, and countless local patriotisms and prejudices, part us among ourselves .... When I am at home, I feel a man from Glasgow to be something like a rival, a man from Barra to be more than half a foreigner. Yet let us meet in some far country, and, whether we hail from the Braes of Manor or the Braes of Mar, some ready-made affections join us on the instant. It is not race. Look at us. One is Norse, one Celtic, another Saxon. It is not the community of tongue. We have it not among ourselves: and we have it almost to perfection with English, or Irish, or American. It is no tie of faith, for we detest each other's errors.'

A good part of Scottish identity springs from the need to accept a common history, as well as a common enemy. In 1286, when Alexander III fell from his horse over a cliff, whilst hurrying home to his new French wife, he set in motion a train of events which did not even end with the union of the crowns

The Scottish fishing industry still survives both in larger towns, such as Buckie on the east coast (top) and in villages such as Lochinver (above left and above far left) on the west coast. However good the catch, there's always enough left for the sea birds. Above: cutting peat near Lock Eriboll in the far nothwest Highlands testifies to the survival of another traditional Scottish industry.

of England and Scotland in 1603. Alexander's heir was his infant granddaughter, the 'Maid of Norway', who died on the voyage back to Scotland. Edward I of England, called in as adviser, adjudicated in his own favour. Having put his personal nominee on the throne, he then tried to batter the Scots into submission. His policy included such refinements as stringing up

Left and far left: twisting the yarn and warping the threads in the manufacture of tweed in Selkirk. Bottom: the wool in its raw state.

The fishing port of Kinlochbervie (above centre left and above centre) in the far northwest has been developed since 1974. The physical remoteness of the district is emphasised by the fact that most of the fishermen return to their homes in the east after landing their catch. Its remoteness from everyday reality is enhanced by reports of mermaids in a bay just to the north. Peat cutters (left and far left) work in bleak surroundings, exposed to the vagaries of the weather.

noblewomen who opposed his regime in cages. It took Robert the Bruce, from whom Queen Elizabeth II is directly descended, fourteen years to re-establish Scottish independence after his swingeing victory at Bannockburn in 1314. A rapprochement seemed to be cemented with the marriage between James IV of Scotland and Margaret Tudor, daughter of Henry VII, but James ruined it in 1513. Under the terms of the 'Auld Alliance' between Scotland and France it had been agreed that, if either country was attacked by England, the other would rally to her support. Thus, when Henry VIII attacked France in 1513, James invaded England. At the subsequent battle of Flodden, Scotland lost her King, most of her leading lights, and her sense of direction. Anglo-Scottish relations were not improved by Elizabeth I's treatment of Mary, Queen of Scots, though the latter had, admittedly, supported the move to disqualify Elizabeth from her throne on the grounds of bastardy and had almost certainly been involved in a plot to assassinate her. James VI of Scotland, and I of England, was the first monarch to rule both countries. The Stuart dynasty ended with his grandson, James II, whose adherence to Catholicism was to be his downfall. For many, the most romantic aspect of Scotland's chequered and bloody history begins, and ends, with the 1745 Rebellion, when Charles Edward Stuart, known as Bonnie Prince Charlie, and grandson of the ousted James II by a second marriage, landed on the west coast of Scotland, unannounced and in disguise, and rallied five thousand Highlanders to his cause. The glory of his failure was the making of the legend.

When the Normans came to Scotland, they came not as invaders, as had been the case in England and Wales, but at the invitation of David I. The introduction of Norman feudalism, however, imposed considerable strain on the clan system, an order which had existed for many generations in the Gaelic-speaking Highlands and under which total obedience was owed to the chief of the clan. To the ordinary clansman, his chief represented the ultimate law of the land, and when the interests of the clan chief conflicted with those of the feudal overlord, or even with those of the king himself,

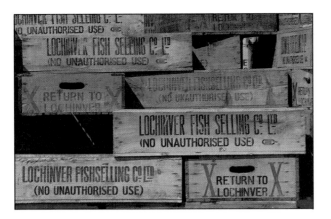

In the northwest of Scotland, both fishermen and sheep have to be hardy to survive. Left: symbols of an undying industry.

Kinlochbervie (above and left), though little more than a harbour, is one of the dozen most important fishing ports in Britain. Together with Aberdeen, Fraserburgh, Lerwick, and Ullapool, it handles some sixty per cent of the total weight of fish landed in Britain.

trouble ensued. The continual disruption of law and order caused by this anomaly, and by the bloody rivalries between individual clans, lasted into the latter half of the eighteenth century, when the Government dismantled the clan system in the aftermath of the 1745 Rebellion to prevent any further revolts. The kinship of the clan was destroyed, but the social fellowship it engendered resurfaced abroad, as the Scots emigrated throughout the world. Boosted by

the establishment of clan societies, it is now as strong as ever. Ironically, individual clan tartans only came to be recognised after the destruction of the clan system, when romantically-minded traditionalists revived, or invented, them. Thus Highland dress as we know it today derives from the nineteenth century. It is customary to attribute the great emigration of Highland Scots in the latter half of the eighteenth century to the introduction of sheep farming from the comparatively prosperous south into the traditionally cattle-raising and small-farming regions of the Highlands. Its roots, however, go much further back, to the period immediately after the break-up of the clan system. Emigration to America is frequently referred to in both Samuel Johnson's and James Boswell's accounts of their tour of the Western Isles of Scotland in 1773. It appears that, even as early as this, the inhabitants of Skye had got positively blasé about going overseas. From Boswell's account: 'We performed, with much activity, a dance which, I suppose, the emigration from Skye has occasioned. They call it America. Each of the couples, after the common involutions and evolutions, successively whirls round in a circle, till all are in motion; and the dance seems intended to show how emigration catches, till a whole neighbourhood is set afloat. Mrs McKinnon told me, that last year when a ship sailed from Portree for America, the people on shore were almost distracted when they saw their relations go off; they lay down on the ground, tumbled, and tore the grass with their teeth.

This year there was not a tear shed.' It has been estimated that between 1771 and 1790 two thousand people emigrated from the sparsely populated island of Skye. In the year 1773 alone, one thousand left the mainland of Inverness to go overseas. Gaelic communities became firmly established in the Americas. Some of the negroes in North Carolina even began to speak Gaelic themselves. This perplexed subsequent immigrants from the Highlands, who concluded that the warmer climate must have caused some of their predecessors to change colour!

The Scots may claim to be the most widely scattered nation in the world. That so many of them

The River Spey (top) is famous for its salmon and attracts fishermen from far and wide. Above: a piper in full Highland dress standing above beautiful Loch Garry. Together they constitute a double tourist attraction. Left: turning the soil, with seagulls in attendance.

in 1616 demanding the establishment of a school in every parish. Robert Burns, one of the very few great poets of the world to have come from an impoverished background, was born in 1759, the eldest son of a poor countryman. Mungo Park, the explorer, who became the first white man to see the river Niger, was born in 1771, the seventh of thirteen children of a

Left: a traditional Highland 'white house' at Kinlochewe. A white house with a thatched roof was known as 'a kind of white house'. A 'black house' was usually made entirely from turf and had no windows.

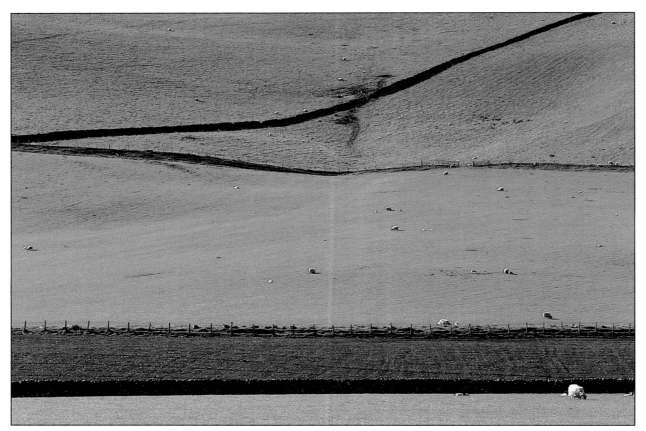

Centre left and top: the spectacular northwest coastline illuminated by stray shafts of sunlight. Above: an oil rig in the Cromarty Firth, an intrusive reminder of how the northeast of Scotland benefited from the discovery in the 1970s of oil and gas under the North Sea. The volatile nature of world oil prices since has had a considerable effect on the economic stability and viability of the region. Left: lowland sheep grazing in the valley of the River Tweed, and (facing page) highland sheep in the northwest. Scotland contains about a third of all the agricultural land in Britain, but sixty-eight per cent of this is comprised of hill grazing.

prospered in their new-found lands was not only due to their pioneering, and often missionary, spirit and an energy born of a healthy respect for hard work and a close acquaintance with hardship. It was also due to an inherent desire for knowledge fostered by an education system which, although rigidly traditional, was more interested in promoting personal development than in maintaining class divisions. The great universities of St Andrews (1411), Glasgow (1451), Aberdeen (1495) and Edinburgh (1583) are older than any others in Britain apart from Oxford and Cambridge. The Scottish Privy Council issued an act

crofter. Both Burns and Park were put through school by their fathers and Park went on to university. In the 1860s, four fifths of Scottish children attended a school. Scottish contributions to science and medical discovery are legion, ranging from the invention of logarithms and calculating machines through the successful development of the steam engine, the discovery of a safe and effective anaesthetic and of penicillin to television. The late flowering of the Scottish spring has had no noticeable effect on the creative genius of the many men and women it has nurtured.

Spring

THE BADMINTON HORSE TRIALS

The equestrian three-day event is not only one of the most difficult of all sports, it is also one of the most hazardous. It has been compared to doing a decathlon on horseback, but even this does not take into account the considerable element of risk to both horse and rider, and the fact that they face a different course each time they compete. The spectators who come to revel in the excitement and suspense and to savour the skills and spills at Badminton each year come also to enjoy the atmosphere and setting of Britain's premier eventing occasion. Lofty Badminton House, seat of the Duke of Beaufort, was built by his ancestor, Henry Somerset (1629-1700), the first Duke. Somerset was a direct descendant of Edward III through the liaison between his fourth son, John of Gaunt, and Catharine Swynford, the children of which were legitimised by Richard II. The first Duke lived at Badminton in considerable style, indulging his passion for hunting, building, and planting. His wife's family were notable gardeners, a tradition which is maintained today by the present Duchess. King William III was entertained at Badminton House in 1690, and Queen Anne in 1702.

Badminton has had notable links with sports other

Facing page: a pause for concentrated refreshment. The show-jumping (top left) and cross-country (top right) phases require completely different dress and equipment. Horsen's Bridge (centre) on the cross-country course incorporates planks and a yawning ditch. The Badminton estate (above and far left) is owned by the Duke of Beaufort (left).

than eventing. It is said to have been here that the game of badminton was invented in the latter half of the nineteenth century. The eighth Duke (1824-99), who was a great sportsman, edited the Badminton Library, that famous collection of definitive sporting tomes. The Badminton Horse Trials have been held here almost every year since 1949. The event was only cancelled in 1987 because of the damage that might have been caused to and by spectators in the aftermath of appalling weather conditions. The prestige and satisfaction of winning at Badminton are enormous in themselves, but the occasion also serves to help the British selectors choose the horses and riders most likely to succeed in any forthcoming international

country. It's like Formula One racing. To do it you've got to have that little bit of stupidity, rather than bravery – and I guess I'm that way inclined!' There is the extra fascination and challenge of how your horse will go on the day, and of pacing and nursing both yourself and your horse through the three days.

Over the whole competition, there is a maximum number of points that can be gained. Marks are deducted for each error and for exceeding the time limit, and the winner is the rider with the fewest penalty points overall. Each horse is required to carry a minimum of eleven stone eleven pounds, so there is no advantage to those with sylph-like figures, as the balance is made up with lead weights, where necessary.

Below: the Duke of Beaufort in the garden of his seventeenth-century home, Badminton House. Bottom left: early morning contemplation and concentration before the dressage. Bottom: through the water at the Lake, a compulsory hazard on the cross-country course.

competitions, in particular the European Championship, the World Championship and the Olympic Games. There have been some memorable winners at Badminton. Lucinda Green, formerly Lucinda Prior-Palmer, has won the event a record six times, whilst Captain Mark Phillips is the only rider to have won in two consecutive years on the same horse, riding Great Ovation to victory in 1971 and 1972. In 1988, Ian Stark came first and second on Sir Wattie and Glenburnie respectively, before going on to win the Olympic silver medal at Seoul.

The origins of the three-day event lie in the training of cavalry horses in obedience, stamina, speed and adaptability and the event itself is the ultimate test of equestrian skill, endurance, and judgment. Virginia Leng, World Champion, triple European Champion, double Olympic bronze medallist and winner at Badminton in 1985, has summed up its attraction thus: 'You have to be good at all three phases – dressage, cross-country, and showjumping. To me, there's that extra appeal of risk in the cross-

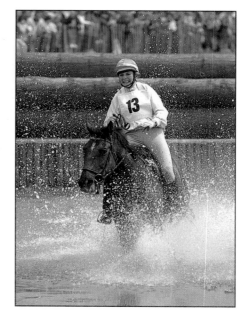

The first of the three days is devoted to dressage, a test of the horse's physique and ability and of the understanding between horse and rider. Twenty separate movements have to be executed from memory. Any error, even if corrected, is penalised by loss of marks, and four errors spells elimination. The demeanour of the horse is taken into account, too. The judges are looking for cheerful mounts as well as sparkling, and immaculately turned-out, riders. One important difference between this and an ordinary dressage competition is that, in order to do itself proper justice on the second day of the three, the horse must be full of energy and power, qualities which could prove detrimental on day one, in the close confines of the dressage ring.

Endurance is the keynote of day two. This phase comprises four distinct and independent stages performed consecutively, with just one ten-minute halt for a veterinary inspection before the last. The total distance of some sixteen miles of roads, tracks, and cross-country has to be covered against the clock in about one and a half hours. In the final phase about

thirty obstacles have to be negotiated whose formidable nature is due entirely to the fiendish ingenuity of their designers. Day two starts with 4,400 metres of roads and tracks to be covered in twenty minutes. A 3,000 metre steeplechase at the gallop follows immediately, the fences being as prescribed by the Jockey Club for its point-to-point races. The steeplechase at Badminton is ridden over a figure-of-eight course whose twists and turns are similar to conditions competitors are likely to encounter on foreign courses. Another 10,000 metres of roads and tracks follows immediately. All but the fittest horses will now be beginning to feel the strain. However, time is always of the essence, and valuable points can be lost by taking too long. The most vital and exhausting stage, the cross-country, is still to come.

Unlike human athletes, horses do not seem to gallop any faster or jump any higher than in past years, and so the maximum permitted height and spread of the obstacles in the cross-country course are the same today as they were when the three-day event

Top: experienced spectators, well equipped. The resident farriers (above) at Badminton still use traditional methods for making horseshoes on the spot. Even at practice (above left), the control required by both horse and rider in the dressage is evident. In the show-jumping phase (below left), the fences are not high, but, with horse and rider both keyed up and tired after the exertions of the previous two days, mistakes are more likely and the slightest touch may topple the bar and result in the deduction of five penalty points.

first featured in the Olympic Games in 1912. Training and riding skills and techniques, on the other hand, have improved, as have the standards of international competition. So new ways are always being devised of increasing the difficulty of the Badminton course, by altering the position of the obstacles in relation to each other and to the natural features of the landscape. The fact that only a handful of riders ever complete the 7,000-metre course within the official time testifies to the problems it poses. Speed between the obstacles is of less significance than the time taken to negotiate each one. Some of them have more than one way of being jumped. One of them, known as the Beefeater Double, has no less than four, depending on whether the rider chooses to be brave, or foolhardy, and fast, or safe but slow. This is where good judgment has to be exercised, to balance the passing of precious

seconds against the chances of a refusal, or even worse, a fall, whilst also taking into account the fitness, and the enthusiasm, of one's horse, and the remaining obstacles. These are obstacles in the truest sense, including banks, bridges, ditches, solid tree trunks, and expanses of water. They have picturesque names, too, which illustrate their nature or provenance: Zig-Zag, Vicarage Open Ditch, Stockholm Fence, Irish Bank, the Lake, Ski Jump, British Equestrian

Olympic Fund Coffin, Woodpile, Quarry, and Huntsman's Hangover, which has to be negotiated as though it were a circus hoop. Even the final obstacle is deliberately uncomfortable, to discourage competitors from looking at their stopwatches instead of concentrating on their riding.

Those horses which survive without being retired or eliminated in one of the earlier phases, or withdrawn on the last morning after failing the compulsory

Elegance is not compulsory when tackling the obstacles on the cross-country course (top left), designed by Lt Col. F.W.C. Weldon (left) the director of the event. Competing horses are guests in Badminton's stables (above and far left), where some feel quite at home thanks to familiar faces. Virginia Leng (facing page top left), World and European Champion, was the first woman ever to win an individual medal in eventing at the Olympic Games. Turn-out for the dressage must be immaculate. Facing page bottom: Vicomte Jurien de la Gravière, President of the Committee of Appeal.

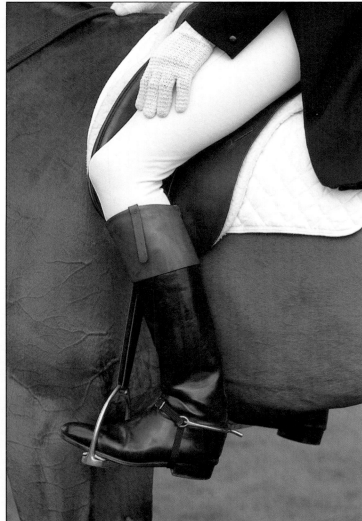

veterinary examination, face the final showjumping competition. After the rigours of the previous day, this is a relatively modest test, but it does demonstrate that the horse is still supple, energetic, and enthusiastic, and also still obedient and capable of exercising the precision necessary to jump the fences. The technique required is very different from the cross-country technique, and many a competition has been won against all the odds when the leading horse and rider, who traditionally jump last in the final phase, inadvertently knock the simplest of fences, letting in the pair who have jumped clear. The pressure is increased in team events, where the slightest personal failure can also make all the difference to the hopes

On the cross-country course, the Lake is approached via a series of three linked obstacles (left). The sponsor's dray (below far left) has been a feature of the event since 1961. Below and below left: a judge, equipped for all eventualities, and (bottom) a spectator in repose.

and aspirations of one's colleagues. The pressure is greater still in competitions such as the Olympic Games, when both individual and team medals are at stake, and to go all out for the one may spell failure in the quest for both.

It takes about four years to train a horse to an acceptable standard in three-day eventing, and the top riders may have as many as ten horses in training at any one time, of which only two or three will be at the required level of skill and experience for competition. Compatibility with the rider is essential. Both may be brilliant individual performers but, like a successful tennis doubles pair, they must also work brilliantly together. The successful rider, apart from sheer talent and determination, needs remarkable powers of touch, timing, and balance, as well as concentration and judgment. There is also the psychological factor. The rider must have icy calm

and self-discipline. Loss of temper means loss of points and a horse which is likely to lack confidence. Also, as Virginia Leng has observed: 'You cannot afford to be conceited. Tomorrow you'll as likely end up flat on your face in the mud! Riders have to be humble people, and learn to take the bad with the good. It's a sport in which it's easy to be a winner, but hard to lose.' She knows the truth of this better than anyone. In 1976, in an appalling fall at a fence during a one-day event, she broke her left arm in twenty-three places. At first, amputation looked likely. Five operations later, the arm had been saved, but it was bent, and the hand was paralysed, all the nerves but one having been crushed when the horse rolled over on her. Yet, thanks to sheer grit, and the attentions of a friendly vet, who looked at the X-rays, took hold of the arm, and yanked it straight, she was competing again just six months after the accident!

Facing page: Badminton faces, Badminton moods, Badminton gear, and Badminton beer, the latter a product of the sponsor. Tension on the face of the rider before the steeplechase and cross-country phases tells all. The stopwatch is a vital part of her equipment.

Spring

RURAL ENGLAND

'It is my belief, Watson, founded upon my experience, that the lowest and vilest alleys of London do not present a more dreadful record of sin than does the smiling and beautiful countryside.' So said Sir Arthur Conan Doyle's detective, Sherlock Holmes, at the end of the last century. Certainly, if one were also to accept the evidence of later English authors of detective novels, such as Dorothy L. Sayers, Agatha Christie, P.D. James, Michael Gilbert, and Ruth Rendell, Holmes's observation would appear to be justifiable. However, the image of the English countryside as a hotbed of crime is not confirmed by the chroniclers of

rural life, from Mary Russell Mitford and Elizabeth Gaskell in the nineteenth century to A.G. Street, Flora Thompson, Adrian Bell, 'Miss Read' and Ronald Blythe in our own. In their writings there is no-one more sinful than the occasional poacher, smuggler, womaniser or burglar, such as Parson Woodforde recalled in the entry in his diary for 1 May 1783: 'The two Fellows who were suspected of breaking open my Stable and many others, were tried this Day at the Sessions at Norwich and convicted of the Robbery of

stealing a Sack from Mr Howlett and are to remain in Prison for three years – which I hope will do good.' Sherlock Holmes and his creator belonged to that pre-commuter era when trains paid regular visits to halts and stops which have long since ceased to serve the community for which they were built. The communities themselves do still exist, but rural England has become a place that people commute from or retire to, rather than the place where they were born, bred, educated, and earn their living. A new breed of country dwellers

Visions of rural England that prove the dream is still a picturesque reality: thatched, colour-washed cottages in Badminton (top left) and Kersey (above), a country pub (top right) and a gently flowing river (above left) in Stratford, and horses grazing in spring meadows near Newbury (centre left).

has emerged, and it is often these commuters and incomers who are the more active environmentalists. On the whole, village architecture has survived better than village institutions and traditions. Thatched roofs and half-timbered frames, and cottage gardens with cobbled paths can still be found. Today's country parson may serve several parishes, but the church is still the most impressive, and probably the most atmospheric, edifice in any village. Sometimes, as in that extraordinary Kentish region of mists and sunsets known since Anglo-Saxon times as Romney Marsh, the medieval churches are virtually the only buildings left. The country church was constructed with great artistry and dedication from the best materials available locally, and thus reflects both the particular crafts that the community excelled in and the materials that the area once supplied. The crafts themselves have largely

disappeared and the local craft shop's stock may come from anywhere! In the churchyard, headstones tell of village history, marking the graves of both rich and poor, and probably of sinners too. The village doctor now conducts his business from some modern small-town block which is designated, mysteriously, a health centre. The manor house, whose owners once supported the community as employers and consumers, is today less a place for living in than for trippers to visit.

Top: the Church of St Mary in Kersey, Suffolk, stands proudly over the village. It was mentioned in the Domesday Book though the present building is largely medieval. Above: an old wooden fingerpost in Wiltshire, one of a dying breed. Left: tourist signs proliferate.

The march of progress and the family motor car, or cars, have spelled the demise of the village shop, that multipurpose emporium cum focal point of the community. Nowadays, if a trip to the supermarket requires too long or too difficult a journey, the travelling shop, like the mobile library, brings goods to the village green if not to the door. The village green itself, if it has not succumbed to the developers, may still provide a local cricket team with an area on which to play. The postman now comes by van. In some areas, the decline of the village school is virtually complete. Families are smaller, and what would be a single-teacher village school with a class of children ranging from six to eleven years old is often considered uneconomic and less than desirable educationally. The most likely institution to have survived is the village pub, but its prosperity today may depend more on modern decor, gin and tonics, piped music, piped beer and bar meals, with ploughman's lunch a speciality and not a ploughman anywhere in sight, than on traditional companionship and traditional ales. The broad sweep of the countryside is most often observed from cars droning monotonously to and fro along the motorways that ribbon the landscape. Rural life is never far away, but it has to be searched out, along the detours, the ancient Roman ways, and the old main and secondary roads. Only those willing to take the time and trouble to go looking will find it.

In Stagsden, Bedfordshire, the village blacksmith (top left) is a rare survival. A mock-Gothic cottage (top) in Badminton epitomises eighteenth-century ideas of rural charm. Horses have been replaced by the car all over England. Horses are too expensive to keep and too slow for the pace of modern life, even in the country.

Left: the rural aspect of industrial England provides a backdrop for identical twins in Houghton-le-Spring, Durham, once a wealthy mining centre and before that a medieval market town. Below: a half-timbered pub in Stratford, once the centre for rural Warwickshire.

least another two centuries after Domesday, but then halted with the dramatic decrease in population after the Black Death in 1349. After about 1600, further cosmetic transformations occurred. Marshes were drained, most notably the East Anglian Fens, the heaths of the Yorkshire Wolds became agricultural land, and common lands were 'enclosed' to make small fields. In the middle of the nineteenth century, some arable land was converted into pasture, creating a broad distinction between the 'grazing counties' in the west of England and the 'corn counties' in the east. The vogue for landscaped gardens and the creation of potato fields and market gardens also modified the countryside. The Industrial Revolution, which began at the end of the eighteenth century, scarred the land with pits, mines, quarries, and huge mounds of waste. Even so, the contrast sometimes drawn between the rural south and the industrial Midlands and north is neither fair nor accurate. Whilst the population in the south continues to increase, there are still vast areas of rural solitude to be found in the north.

The village of Kersey (above left) has developed along its single main street. The village gave its name to a type of woollen cloth which was originally manufactured there by Flemish weavers. Village cricket flourishes from late spring onwards on rural pitches all over England. A Sunday afternoon game at Brook (above) in Surrey gives a representative picture.

The poet William Cowper wrote in 1783, 'God made the country and man made the town', but by the time the Normans invaded in 1066, the countryside had already been developed by human effort into regions and settlements. The survey carried out in 1086 that resulted in the Domesday Book names over 13,000 English settlements and reveals a land even then divided into the shires, or counties, which remained intact until the twentieth century. Most of their names still survive. The character of the English countryside had been determined before the writing of the Domesday Book, and the changes wrought over the years since have altered it only superficially. Reclamation of land from the forests went on for at

~ Britain and Her People ~

· CHAPTER 2 ·

SUMMER

Matthew Arnold referred to 'all the live murmur of a summer's day'. Summer's murmurs, for the inquisitive traveller in Britain, may include the roar of the World War I fighter rebuilt by Doug Gregory (above), the rustle of Warwickshire folk-dancers' dresses (below) or the hum of satisfied insects in a Cotswold garden (right).

AN OXFORD *Spring* COMMEMORATION BALL

'And that sweet City with her dreaming spires, She needs not June for beauty's heightening'. The lines are Matthew Arnold's, from the poem *Thyrsis*, an elegy written on the death of his friend, Arthur Hugh Clough, in 1861. The city is, of course, Oxford, whose skyline of towers and pinnacles, domes and cupolas, and, of course, spires, still survives, courtesy of Oxford City Council. Since 1962, the Council has banned any

new building over sixty feet high within a central area, and also between that area and six designated viewpoints around the city perimeter. It may be true, as Arnold goes on to suggest, that June can do nothing to embellish this panorama of a thriving, bustling city housing an ancient centre of academic excellence and of dignified calm. It is, however, in June of each year that that dignified calm is shattered, as college buildings reverberate to the sounds of all-night dance bands, to the beat of jazz and pop music and to the whirr and thump of fairground machinery. For June is the month when the university's many benefactors are commemorated. It also marks the end of the academic year, when about a third of the undergraduates will have finished their studies and sat their final examinations. Those who have the money to spend on a double ticket and can drum up a partner with the necessary staying power may choose to celebrate

Top right: the hall and cathedral of Christ Church College contribute to the 'dreaming spires' of Oxford. Top left: Oriel College Commemoration Ball – opening gambits played against a backdrop of roses. Well-chilled champagne (above), ice cream (far left) or a breath of night air (left) all provide a chance to cool off once the ball is under way. Facing page: punting on the River Cherwell, a favourite daytime pursuit. By tradition, Oxford men manage the pole from the open, sloping part at the back of the boat, and not from the flat end that appears to be its stern.

amidst the glitter of one of several college Commemoration Balls. These follow the college balls held in May to celebrate Eights Week, a rowing festival which culminates in riotous 'bump suppers' for the successful crews and elaborate practical jokes, some calling for considerable engineering skill.

The view that being at Oxford, or Cambridge for that matter, is simply participating in a continual social and sporting whirl is erroneous. It would be equally erroneous to believe, however, that those who have concentrated solely on their studies and on gaining a good final result have fully benefited from the system. Oxford offers a multitude of cultural and sporting activities which can be indulged in at the highest levels

By the time the 'survivors' photograph' (above) is taken at 6.00 a.m. in Oriel Square, shawls or partners' jackets are essential wear for women, to ward off the early morning chill. Left: it was easier to smile earlier in the proceedings.

thing for those who have come straight to university from single-sex schools. Unusually, the tutorial system is also college based, so it is the individual college and not the university that organises and provides the tuition, which is supplemented by voluntary attendance at university lectures. Despite all the non-academic opportunities available, this system cannot be abused with impunity. Nemesis is not slow to strike even the most justified of backsliders, and it is good that from time to time the insistence of both Oxford and Cambridge on maintaining academic standards makes the newspapers, even if only the sports' pages. In recent years a captain of each university's cricket team has been been forbidden in one case to return, in the other to play, because of insufficient progress in his studies. A key batsman was refused permission by the authorities to take an examination on another day, which would have released him to play for the Combined Universities cricket side, who were fighting for a place in the semifinals of the Benson and Hedges Cup. The

Below: the calm of the brasserie tent in the first quadrangle. The tent has a real French flavour, serving Orangina, coffee, and mineral water as well as wine. From 3.00 a.m. there's even 'petit déjeuner', a continental breakfast, for those who can stomach it. The ball is spread over three quadrangles, and several activities are offered in each throughout the night, plus a continuous cabaret. Few couples attempt to savour even half the attractions on offer.

Left: food and drink offer the opportunity to recharge one's batteries whilst strolling round the quad. Above: emerging from the jazz cellar under the glare of coloured lights.

and which can broaden the student's experience and sharpen his or her awareness of life. The Oxford Union is a debating society of international renown. Many notable actors, actresses, and musicians have been guided towards their future careers through college dramatic clubs and university musical societies. University drama groups perform at international festivals and college choirs give concerts overseas. The social life is what you make of it. There is no campus, so students usually live in their particular college for their first two years, and then in approved lodgings for their third and any subsequent years. All but two of the colleges, both all female, are now mixed. Apart from the academic advantages, this is undoubtedly a good match was lost, by a hair's-breadth!

Within living memory, however, sporting prowess was a factor taken into account by some colleges when considering applicants, and one notable cricketer, who was nominally reading Geography, took extended leave in the middle of his final year to play for England in Australia, and never reappeared. Even further back, sportsmen were actively solicited by both universities, whose rivalry in sports is the subject of national and international interest and partisanship. It is said that one such applicant, noted for his brawn rather than his brain, was called for interview. 'Would you tell us,' he was asked as soon as he had sat down, 'who was the first king of Israel and Judah?' There was a long silence while the young man struggled with the question and the panel waited expectantly. Finally, 'Saul?', he offered tentatively. The panel expelled its corporate breath. 'Thank you, thank you, Mr —,' said the chairman, 'that will be quite sufficient. Congratulations to you.' The sportsman rose and walked to the door. When he reached it, he turned, with his hand on the knob. 'Afterwards called Paul,' he observed, with a beatific smile.

For a Commemoration Ball, men still dress as formally as ever, although black and, heaven forfend, coloured ties and soft collars are now acceptable.

breakfast to those who can face it. Dodgems, side-shows and videos provide further entertainment, while more unusual items may include a massage parlour, a fortune-teller, a confessional box, and a scalectrix race track. A face painter may offer to alter the appearance of guests' features, artistically of course. Security is strict, and gate-crashers, including the pantomime

From animated beginnings (facing page top left) the long evening wears the merrymakers down to an eventual standstill (facing page bottom centre). Christ Church College's main gate (facing page top right) is perfect for grand entrances.

Top left: varieties of fashion – white satin, worn with elegance; traditional kilt, worn with manic glare; and braided dinner jacket, worn with scarlet tie and cummerbund. Formality has relaxed (above) by early morning. Top: post mortem amid the debris! Left: 6.30 a.m. by the clock on Carfax Tower, and it's the end of a perfect night. The sun has risen over Oxford High Street as the revellers return home.

Female hairstyles may have changed little over the years, but their dress has, often in favour of more daring styles.

It takes about eighteen months to organise a Commemoration Ball. The extravagant, multifarious entertainment goes on all night, in marquees, in quadrangles, on the lawns, and in all available parts of the college buildings. There is dancing to a choice of three different bands and a disco. There will be a college revue and a professional cabaret. A four-course dinner is served to those who want it, and

horse which tried to gain entrance to the Magdalen Commemoration Ball a few years ago, are sent courteously on their way. To fail to enjoy oneself can be quite a disaster, especially given the high price of tickets, but a night in a noisy crowd is not always conducive to romance, and the weather cannot be guaranteed either. Yet some positively revel in the atmosphere. After one night of particularly vile weather, a couple were asked at six o'clock the next morning if they had had a good time, in spite of the rain. 'Rain?' they replied. 'We thought it was champagne.'

Summer

SUNDAY AT COVENT GARDEN

In the history of modern urban development it is rare to find a part of England's valued heritage that has outgrown its old usefulness being given a new lease of life rather than being completely redeveloped. Yet this is what has happened in Covent Garden, in the heart of one of London's busiest districts. The area, which was originally owned by the Russell family, whose town house stood nearby in the Strand, was the site of the first planned urban development in London. At first the scheme fell foul of the dreaded Star Chamber, which threatened a suit for a contravention of the

Performing in the old market (top left) may give some artistes their first taste of live audience reaction (top right). Above left: touting for tourist business, a photographer and his prop. Above: staying cool. Away from London's traffic, Covent Garden pedestrians sit and watch the world go by. The Sunday market (left) in the transformed shopping precinct always attracts bargain hunters. Once a place where fruit and flowers were sold wholesale, the old market is now the site of smart boutiques and Sunday picnics (facing page).

proclamation against new buildings. And that was in 1630! The instigator of the scheme was Francis Russell (1593-1641), fourth Earl of Bedford. In 1630 he commissioned the architect and stage designer Inigo Jones (1573-1652), surveyor of works to the royal family, to build an Italianate open piazza on the Covent Garden site.

The development was to include a church, for which the parsimonious Earl suggested that 'something like a barn' would suffice. The upshot was St Paul's Church, Covent Garden, the grandest barn in Europe,

plain but majestic, which is today the chapel of the theatrical fraternity, where many famous actors, and also artists, are buried. By the time of the Restoration in 1660, the development was almost completed, but still lacked the two elements for which it was to become famous. Then, in 1670, Charles II granted a licence for what had been a few temporary stalls to become a formal market, opening every day of the week except Sunday, throughout the year. Next, with the revival of the theatre after its suppression by the Puritans and the return of actors, writers and theatrical devotees, the Theatre Royal was built in Drury Lane. The present threatre, built in the early years of the nineteenth century, is the fourth building on the site. In the first one, Nell Gwynn (1650-87), mistress to Charles II, sold oranges, before being elevated from the pit to the stage in 1665, when she played in *The Indian Emperor* by John Dryden (1631-1700). This building burned down in 1672. Its replacement, designed by Sir Christopher Wren (1632-1723), witnessed performances by all the top actors and actresses of the

day, as well as an assassination attempt on George II in 1716. The third theatre on the site was managed by Richard Brinsley Sheridan (1751-1816), Irish dramatist and Whig politician. He was a chronic alcoholic, whose policy of 'borrow and fear not' caused him endless trouble. That theatre burned down in 1809. As Sheridan watched the conflagration, a friend commented on his equanimity. 'A man may surely be allowed to take a glass of wine by his own fireside,' he replied. The nearby Covent Garden Theatre was begun in 1731. It burned down, an occupational hazard for theatres in the eighteenth and nineteenth centuries, in 1808 and 1856, being redesigned on the latter occasion as the Royal Opera House, Covent

Garden, which is to this day one of the great opera houses of the world. The rivalry between the Theatre Royal and the Covent Garden Theatre reached its height in 1750-51 with Shakespeare's *Romeo and Juliet* running at the same time in both. From a very early date, Covent Garden was a haunt of the literary and the fashionable. The diarist, Samuel Pepys (1633-1703) stopped off there one evening in 1664 and found 'very witty and pleasant discourse' in the coffee house, among a gathering which included the poet and dramatist, John Dryden, and 'all the wits of the town'.

Another self-confessed libertine who recorded a visit to Covent Garden was James Boswell (1740-95), the biographer of Samuel Johnson. One Sunday in

Top: walking out – two much-decorated members of the Normandy Veterans Association in front of the modern version of the Stuart and Georgian coffee-shops. Above: riding out – cyclists take a break. Street theatre (facing page), professional or incidental, is at the heart of the new Covent Garden.

1763, while in the act of seducing the actress Louisa Lewis in her bedroom, he was disturbed by the entrance of her brother. In his confusion, Boswell recalled that he had not been to church that day, and 'begged pardon for a little and went to Covent Garden Church', returning afterwards for family tea and polite conversation. By the late eighteenth century, congestion and controversy were already beginning to affect the smooth running of the market. A hundred years later, an observer recorded that on a summer morning 'The surrounding streets are choked with waggons and

barrows ... The porters amble in all directions under loads of prodigious bulk .... Within the market enclosure the stacks of vegetables, and the piles of fruit baskets and boxes, are of startling extent.' That was in 1872. The celebrated fruit and vegetable market continued to multiply next door to the celebrated opera house for another hundred years, while people and Parliament argued about separating them and relieving the congestion. What would replace the market as a traditional focus? As David Piper, Director of the

Ashmolean Museum, Oxford, wrote, 'Whatever it is had better be good, for Covent Garden, as a market, is a quality of London that is going to be sorely missed.' The old market building is now a well-used shopping and leisure precinct. Designers and publishers occupy the houses and redundant warehouses. What of the market itself? Since 1974 it has been on the other side of the River Thames, on a purpose-built site by Vauxhall Bridge. In the time it has been there, its turnover has more than trebled!

Top left: a visual message for the public and (top right) an aural message for the young. Above and above left: folk performers and their audience. Facing page: not everybody gives the the new Covent Garden their unqualified approval.

Summer

TROOPING THE COLOUR

Her Majesty the Queen's official birthday in early June is celebrated with a dazzling exhibition of marching and counter-marching by massed military bands and infantry battalions. It is an exhibition that illustrates the British devotion to traditional display and military precision. The occasion is called Trooping the Colour and is derived from a ceremony originally designed to familiarise troops with their regimental standard before battle. Each year, one of the infantry regiments that form the Household Division does the main honours on Horseguards Parade before a crowd of some seven thousand, with millions more watching on television. As the Queen, attended by a guard of the Household Cavalry and by the mounted band of the Sovereign's

Top left: troops line the Mall along the route from Buckingham Palace to Horseguards Parade. Behind them stand the flag-waving public in a show of patriotic pride (top right and above centre). Centre left: HM the Queen takes the salute from a specially constructed dais. Left: troopers of the Household Cavalry; the Blues and Royals, wearing red plumes, are followed by the Life Guards, wearing white plumes. Above: special dress, too, for the mounted police. Facing page: HM the Queen returns to the Palace. Behind her are the senior officers, on horseback, and the infantry of the Household Division, of which she is Colonel-in-Chief.

Escort, arrives at precisely 11 a.m., the chimes of Big Ben ring out, there is a massive single crunch of boots as the waiting troops come to attention and present arms, and from nearby Hyde Park a royal salute of forty-one guns is fired. Having inspected the lines of troops from her carriage, the Queen mounts the ceremonial dais to await the trooping of the massed bands. The bands perform a series of complicated manoeuvres first in slow and then in quick time, playing as they march. Then a single drummer gives

the call to begin the trooping of the colour itself. While the massed bands execute their marvellous spin-wheel, the ensign carrying the standard marches, with an escort, along the ranks, showing the flag as they go. They then take their place in the grand march-past, which is executed first at a slow march and then again at the normal quick pace. Finally it is the turn of the sovereign's escort itself, which marches past, led by the pipers of the Scots and Irish Guards and followed by the drum horses and the massed bands.

Summer

DERBY DAY, EPSOM

Epsom is famous for the broad sweeps and springy turf of its downs, for its race course, which hosts two classic races, the Oaks and the Derby, and for its salts. In 1618, a farmer called Henry Wicker stumbled upon or, by some accounts, into a spring of curious-tasting water whose true medicinal properties were not discovered for some years. Then, the place became a popular resort for the fashionable from London. Samuel Pepys records a visit on 14 July 1667: 'Taking some bottles of wine and beer and some cold fowle with us into the coach, we took coach and four horses which

I had provided last night, and so away — a very fine day; and so towards Epsum, talking all the way pleasantly. The country was very fine; only, the way very dusty. We got to Epsum by 8 a-clock to the Well, where much company; and there we light and I drank the water; they did not, but do go about and walk a little among the women, but I did drink four pints…' While the town gave its name to the preparation still known as Epsom Salts, the wells from which the mineral substance derived were abandoned or closed early in the eighteenth century in an atmosphere which suggested that there had been some fraudulent

commercial practices.

Henry VIII first saw the possibilities of the area as a sporting and leisure centre, building Nonsuch Palace at Epsom as a sort of vast holiday home. James I, who was a passionate follower of, and participant in, horse racing, was certainly a frequent visitor to Nonsuch Palace during his reign, but the earliest recorded horse race on the Downs was not until 1648. This was, in fact, merely a thoroughly ingenious cover for a conference of royalist supporters plotting to restore Charles I to his throne during the Civil War. The first race meeting proper seems to have been the one held

This page: the car park as social centre. Here people gather to shelter from the wind, be converted by one of the missions which have always attended Derby Day, swap hats or restore their energies with refreshments. Charabancs and open-top buses have served as grandstands since the 1920s.

on 7 March 1661, in the presence of Charles II, to celebrate the Restoration. In May 1663, Samuel Pepys was intending to go to the races at Epsom but the meeting was postponed for a couple of days, by which time he was preoccupied with other matters. However he did record that at the postponed meeting there was 'a great throng' on the Downs.

Regular competitions and race meetings at Epsom began in the early years of the eighteenth century. In June 1774, Edward Stanley, who succeeded his grandfather in 1776 to become twelfth Earl of Derby, brought his fiancée, Elizabeth Hamilton, to celebrate their engagement at 'The Oaks', a country house which he had recently bought on Epsom Downs. The family had long had widespread horseracing interests from and, as a member of the Jockey Club, Stanley was appointed Honorary Steward of the Epsom races.

As a direct result of this connection, the Oaks Stakes, a race restricted to three-year-old fillies, was established in 1779 as the highlight of the May meeting. The first race, which was won, appropriately, by Lord Derby's own horse, got little publicity, but its backers readily agreed to repeat the experiment the following year. The race has been held ever since. Another race was envisaged to enliven the 1780 meeting, also for three year olds, but to include colts as well as fillies. When it came to naming the race, two of its most prominent sponsors spun a coin for the honour.

The two participants in this friendly competition to

Above: a badge of office holds down a symbol of celebration. Left: the odds look better from the bonnet of a Bentley.

DERBY DAY, EPSOM

choose a name for the new race were Lord Derby and Sir Charles Bunbury, President of the Jockey Club. Derby won, and thus gave his name to the Derby Stakes, now the world's most prestigious flat race. The first Derby was run on Thursday, 4 May 1780. It was won by the favourite, Sir Charles Bunbury's Diomed, ridden by Sam Arnull, over one mile. In 1784, the distance was extended to one-and-a-half miles, which it has remained to this day. The day's sport also included an inter-county cock fight between birds owned and trained by gentlemen from Middlesex, Surrey and Wiltshire. Thus began the tradition of the Derby as a big day out. By 1793, *The Times* was

famous illustrations of London in 1872: 'On the Derby morning, all London wakes at cock-crow. The first flicker of light breaks upon thousands of busy men in misty stables: breaks upon a vast encampment of the Romans' [i.e. Romanies, or gypsies] 'and other less reputable wandering tribes on the Downs; breaks upon lines of loaded pedestrians footing it from London, to turn a penny on the great event. Horsey folk issue from every beer-shop and inn on the road. The beggars are in mighty force; the tattered children take up their stations. Who wants to see samples of all degrees of Cockneys, has his golden opportunity to-day. From the Heir Apparent, with his handsome,

Below: informal hairstyles and formal top hats in the paddock. Outside the paddock, informal and semi-formal meet (bottom left). Bottom right: 'All men are equal – all men, that is to say, who possess umbrellas.' (E.M.Forster, Howards End, ch. 6)

reporting: 'The road to Epsom was crowded with all description of people hurrying to the races, some to plunder and some to be plundered. Horses, gigs, curricles, coaches, chaises, carts and pedestrians covered with dust crowded the Downs, the people running down and jostling each other as they meet in contact.' The newspaper reported even greater distress in 1795: 'Several carriages were broken to pieces, and one lady had her arm broken. There was much private business done in the swindling way. One black-legged fellow cleared near a thousand pounds by the old trick of an E.O. table [a shady form of roulette]. Another had a faro table, and was on the eve of doing business, when he was detected with a palmed card: almost the whole of what may be justly styled the "vagabond gamblers" of London were present.' On top of this, 'Upwards of thirty carriages were robbed coming home from the races.' Whatever the hazards of the journey home, the extraordinary exodus from London on Derby day became a nationally recognised phenomenon. As Blanchard Jerrold joyously records in the text he wrote to accompany Gustav Doré's

manly English face, to the vilest of Fagin's pupils; the observer may pass all our Little Villagers in review. The sharp-faced, swaggering betting man; the trim, clean groom with a flower in his button-hole; the prosperous, heavy-cheeked tradesman; the ostentatious clerk; the shambling street singer; the hard, coarse-visaged costermonger; the pale and serious artisan; the frolicsome apprentice in flaming neck-tie; the would-be aristocrat flashing his silver mug of foaming Roederer in the eyes of the Vulgar packed as close as pigs in a butcher's cart … . If you desire to see the fresh buxom wives and daughters of the lower middle class, dight in their ideas of the fashion; if you wish to study the outward belongings of the workman's spouse and girl; if you would get a true idea of the apple-woman, the work-girl in holiday finery, the beggar's female companion, in a cart with Dick Swiveller and his pals – and all in the highest spirits, now is your opportunity; and it will last clear all through the day, and even a fair stretch into the night.' The 'Heir Apparent' was the future Edward VII, who was not only a great racing

Whether you win or lose on the race itself, you can enjoy the off-course entertainment (top and above), which is often as lavish and exotic as the surrounding fashions. Above left and below left: for the punter there is ample literature available, but it does not guarantee results. The winner on the day was HH the Aga Khan's Kahyasi, ridden by R. Cochrane, which came in at 11-1.

enthusiast, but also the owner of three Derby winners, Persimmon in 1896, Diamond Jubilee in 1900, and Minoru in 1909, by which time Edward was king. The intermingling of the classes was a feature of the Derby. 'Strolling amid the booths and tents we find elbowing each other, bantering, playing, drinking, eating and smoking; shoals of shop-boys and clerks, tradesmen in fast attire, mechanics in holiday dress, wondering foreigners, gaudy ladies, generally of loud voice and unabashed manner. We come upon a noble earl indulging in three throws for a penny. He has been recognised by a few bystanders; and the whisper that a peer is casting sticks at cocoanuts and dolls has travelled apace.' One of the 'wondering foreigners' who attended the Derby at this time was the French literary critic and historian Hippolyte Taine. He recorded his impressions of the race itself: 'To the eye the speed is not very great; it is that of a railway train seen at the distance of half a league. During several minutes, the brown patch, strewn with red and bright spots, moves steadily over the distant green. It turns; one perceives the first group approach. A suppressed

hurrah pervades the stands. The frigid faces are on fire; brief, nervous gestures suddenly stir the phlegmatic bodies. Below, in the betting ring, the agitation is extraordinary – like a general St Vitus's dance …'.

Whilst the general ambience of the Derby may have been cleaned up in the intervening years, its excitement, holiday atmosphere and astonishing mix of followers remain unchanged today. As far as the race itself is concerned, it has had its share of sensational incidents as well as of sensational winners. In 1880, Fred Archer, riding with one arm in a metal splint, came from behind in the last furlong to win, on Bend Or. A subsequent objection that his declared mount was actually a completely different horse was unsuccessful and the result stood. In 1884, the favourite was withdrawn when its owner died of overexcitement at Newmarket, and the final result was only the second dead heat in the history of the race. In 1904, two spectators were struck by lightning. The 1913 race

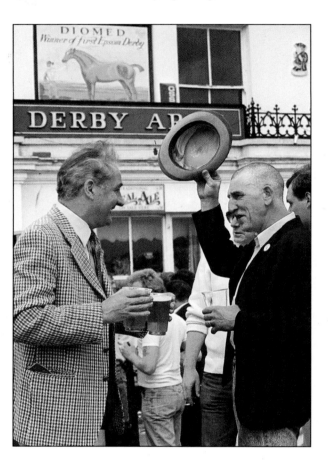

The many facets of Derby Day. Top left: greeting friends at the pub, (top right) reflecting on the odds in the car park, (left) chatting in the paddock and (above) grand entrance!

Left: HM the Queen, herself a notable racehorse owner, walks round the paddock before the race. Below: the tension mounts.

saw both tragedy and sensation. As the field raced through Tattenham Corner, the suffragette Emily Davison ran into the path of the following group, bringing down the colt owned by King George V. The horse and its jockey recovered, but Emily died in hospital four days later, without regaining consciousness. The leading riders, unaware of the accident, had pushed on. First past the post was the favourite, Craganour, who appeared to push Aboyeur onto the rails. However, the result was confirmed and bookmakers reluctantly started to pay out. Then came an objection, not from Aboyeur's owner or jockey, but from the stewards themselves. Craganour was ultimately

disqualified, and Aboyeur declared the winner, at odds of 100-1! There was another rough race in 1952, when the young Lester Piggott on Gay Time came off worst in a barging match with Tulyar, which went on to win, with Gay Time ditching its unfortunate jockey at the post. Piggott, however, went on to ride a record nine Derby winners between 1954 and 1983. In 1962, Larkspur won a race in which no fewer than seven horses fell. Even though it meant beating the Queen's horse in her coronation year, the most popular win ever was by miner's son Gordon Richards, knighted only a few days before the race. Riding Pinza, he achieved the only Derby victory of a career in which he seldom failed to become champion jockey, and then usually because of injury.

The Derby, begun in an informal way by a group of aristocratic enthusiasts, has retained its attraction and its eccentricity for well over two hundred years. Neither television nor traffic jams have dimmed the appeal of the occasion, nor people's obvious enjoyment in simply being there.

Familiar faces. Gypsies (above left) have always made the Derby a major meeting point for their people, and acted for years as self-appointed car park attendants, as well as being tipsters and flower sellers. Left: members of the Women's Royal Voluntary Service who have been officiating at the Derby for fifteen years. Tom Smith (above) has been a valued attendant for twenty-six years.

Summer

POLO AT WINDSOR

Polo was being played in Persia over two thousand years ago. The earliest account of an international match, between teams of Persians and Turks, is in an eleventh-century manuscript. The Mongol conqueror, Genghis Khan (1162-1227), favoured a game with a thousand players per side, whilst the Tartar, Tamerlane (1336-1405), used his enemies' heads as polo balls.

Later the game became popular with Indian maharajahs. It came to Britain in 1869 when officers of the 10th Regiment of Hussars, having read about it in a magazine, tried out their own version using a billiard ball and hockey sticks. The requisites for a regular player in modern times are a good eye, a strong arm, a safe seat, at least four trained ponies, and a substantial income. A team consists of four players, each of whom is awarded a handicap according to his value to the team, assessed as a number of goals, from minus two to plus ten. Over the last century, there have been no more than sixty-five ten-goal handicap players in the world. A match consists of four or five chukkas, each lasting seven and a half minutes. Unlimited equine substitutions are allowed in this fast and bruising game.

Top left: the ball isn't always where you think! In a fast and furious game, the pauses between chukkas provide a welcome rest and a chance to discuss tactics (top right). HRH the Prince of Wales (far left and above), is an enthusiastic four-handicap player. Centre and left: loyal supporters. Facing page: in the melee, protection for both horses and riders is essential.

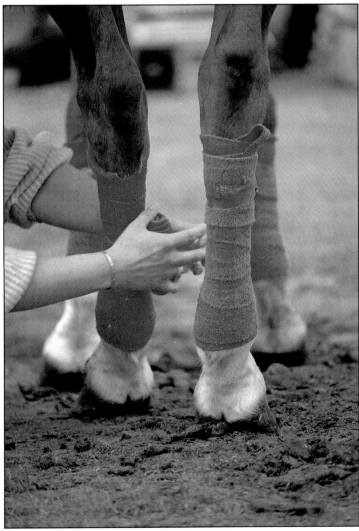

Summer

THE BRITISH NANNY

Ever since the time and place so vividly, if romantically, recreated by Rodgers and Hammerstein in *The King and I*, the nanny has been one of Britain's most influential visible exports. Her popularity still flourishes, to judge by the testimony of one Norland-trained nurse: 'I trained ten years ago and since then have worked and travelled in many countries around the world, such as Sri Lanka, Hong Kong, China, Thailand, Burma, Malaysia, Singapore, Bali, Australia, the Pacific Islands, and New Zealand. When I started at Norland, my dream was to travel the world, so, as you can see, dreams do come true! My next destination is America.' There appear to be, overall, three times as many vacancies as there are qualified nannies to fill them.

The Norland Nursery Training College was founded in 1892. It was the brainchild of Mrs Emily Ward, an early advocate of the system of child education evolved by Friedrich Froebel (1782-1852), which uses instructive play and encourages spontaneous development. In 1837, Froebel opened the first kindergarten near Blankenburg, and he devoted the rest of his life to the organisation of further establishments of this kind and to the training of

Facing page: still and animated life beneath a portrait of the founder of Norland Nursery Training College, Mrs Emily Ward. Much of a nanny's time is spent pushing prams or buggies, so practice makes for perfect professionalism. Above: a bevy of Norland trainees lines up ready for the off. Far left: 'But I'm sure we had three last time we looked!' Left: 'I knew there was a right way up.'

suitable teachers to staff them.

Mrs Ward's methods and standards helped to change, though not, for many years, to destroy, the traditional image of the starch-fronted disciplinarian so affectionately recalled and parodied by Joyce Grenfell: 'Nanny knows best'; 'You must wear clean underwear, you might get run over'; 'A dose of good syrup is what you need'; etc. Since 1967, the college has occupied the impressive complex of Georgian mansion and ancillary buildings in hundred-acre Denford Park in Berkshire. Facilities include a computer room and a day nursery with a permanent stock of some twenty children on whom students can practise

Tender loving care (left) is as important as encouraging constructive play (below left). Below: learning to drive with care.

Left: Louise E. Davis, Principal of Norland College, with some of her uniformed charges. Above: in the classroom. The college undertakes continuous assessment of the students' theoretical studies as well as of their practical work, which teaches them to cope with both routine situations and potential emergencies. Facing page: on the job training, taking real children for a walk in the park!

the skills they are taught. The course lasts two years and concentrates on the care and health of children, the personal development of each student, and social skills, such as cooking. Practical work is undertaken in playgroups and primary schools, and in the children's and maternity wards of local hospitals. Passing the necessary examinations is not the end of the course, however. Nine months must then be spent in an approved probationary post before the coveted Norland Diploma is gained. The college has sporting facilities

and organises social and cultural events. Students are positively encouraged to bring their own cars, or at least to take driving lessons, since a driving licence is an asset when applying for a post as a children's nurse. Times are changing in other ways. The Equal Opportunities Commission has already had to adjudicate in the case of a young man whose application to become a nanny was rejected on the grounds of his sex. How long will it be before Norland College has to allow lads as well as lasses through its doors?

Summer

A SOUTH COAST SUMMER

Summer is the best time to take a sailing trip around England's south coast. Setting out from the north coast of Kent, there is little point in dropping anchor at Whitstable in search of its oysters, famous for their tastiness and size, as these delicious molluscs are not in season over the summer months. Herne Bay, a little further along the north Kent coast, is a resort offering

a shingle and pebble beach and the second longest pier in England. A mile inland lies the village of Herne and its fourteenth-century church, where the incumbent at one time was a Nicholas Ridley (c.1500-55). This priest had the Te Deum sung in English for the first time, which did not go down well with his masters. He became chaplain to Henry VIII and, in 1547, Bishop of Rochester. He was eventually condemned to death by Queen Mary for heresy, although his actual crime was supporting the cause of Lady Jane Grey as Queen. Ridley was burnt at the stake in Oxford, commenting, 'Farewell Herne, thou worshipful and wealthy parish'. Following the coast, the sailor rounds the North and South Forelands into the Channel, that strip of sea

The choice of British seaside pursuits is often dictated by the weather. A brisk walk along the cliff tops at Beachy Head or a warming game of bowls on the front at Hastings are just as likely as an ice cream on the front at Weymouth. However, some visitors to the latter resolutely refuse to shed their clothing whatever the weather. A visit to Brighton pier, playing in the sand in Weymouth or a quiet nap in Herne Bay are all viable alternatives.

which separates Britain from the rest of Europe.

Keeping the coast to the right, or starboard, side, the five original Cinque Ports heave into view. Their function until the end of the fifteenth century was to provide the ships and men to ward off invasion. Hastings is the westernmost of these. The so-called Battle of Hastings in 1066 was actually fought six miles inland, at Battle, but William the Conqueror did choose Hastings as the headquarters of his fleet and army after the sixty-mile crossing from St Valéry. He is also said to have dined at Hastings before the battle, using a giant stone as a table. The stone, if the tradition is true, is the one now displayed by the promenade, near the pier. An historical event which definitely did take place

Left: deckchair study on a deserted beach at Brighton, and (below left) the diverse architecture of Brighton's seafront, seen from Palace Pier, which was completed in 1899. The West Pier, built in 1866, is no longer open to the public.

Above centre: contemplating the beach at Selsey, one hot weekend in June. Left: early evening in Swanage, and no one seems to want to leave the shelter on the promenade. Above: a traditional Brighton pursuit, more usually practised in private, and beyond, another perennial seaside game: retrieving chairs from the sea.

in Hastings was the first ever television transmission, made, in 1924, by the eccentric Scottish inventor John Logie Baird (1888-1946) in a tiny, dingy attic room above a flower shop in present-day Queen's Avenue. Baird had been sent to the south coast to recuperate from illness. His first Hastings experiment was an ever-sharp glass razor blade, with which he cut himself so badly that he ended up in hospital. Farther along the Sussex coast, past Beachy Head, lies Brighton.

This was discovered as a resort by the future King George IV in 1783, when he was Prince of Wales, and the town became famous for its royal patronage, Regency architecture, quaint back streets and discreet accommodation for lovers. The Royal Pavilion was originally designed for the Prince of Wales as a classical-style seaside residence, the interior decorated throughout in elaborate Chinese style. When George became Prince Regent, the exterior was remodelled by

John Nash (1752-1835), architect of Buckingham Palace, in Indian Moghul style, with minarets, pinnacles, and onion-shaped domes, retaining the Chinese atmosphere within. Brighton today is an extraordinary mixture of the tasteful, the picturesque, the extravagant, the functional and the commercially brash. Sailing on past Bognor, where the International Clowns' Convention is held every spring, Selsey is reached. This was once an island, on which stood a pre-Norman cathedral, long ago washed away by the sea. Passing the Isle of Wight, the sailor arrives in the gigantic natural harbour of Poole, where a detour up either the River Frome or the Piddle, also called the Trent, leads to the historic town of Wareham, situated between the two rivers. Wareham was Dorset's chief port from Saxon times until the Middle Ages. During the Civil War, the town repeatedly changed hands between the Cavaliers and the Roundheads. After the rebellion of the Duke of Monmouth (1649-85) against his uncle, James II, Wareham was one of the towns, in which Judge Jeffreys (1648-89) held the so-called 'Bloody Assizes' to try the rebels. St Martin's Church, the

oldest church in Dorset, contains an effigy of T.E. Lawrence (1888-1935), the desert leader who, under the alias of Aircraftsman Shaw, was stationed nearby until his death in a motorcycle accident.

Weymouth is the final stopping point on this trip. Situated on a broad bay, with sandy beaches, a harbour and a naval base, Weymouth claims to have witnessed the first bathing machine in operation in 1763. In 1789, George III was inveigled into trying out this newfangled contraption, while the band played 'God save the King'. He thus became the first reigning British monarch to indulge in sea-bathing. Weymouth's Georgian architecture shows the effect which this event had on the town's development and prosperity.

It is still possible to enjoy quiet moments at the seaside, whether on the beach in Brighton (top left) or reading the Sunday papers in Herne Bay (top). Above: the end of a tranquil summer's day at Wareham's inland harbour. Left: the Thames estuary surveyed from a hill above Herne Bay.

Summer

A KENTISH IDYLL

Kent is known as the 'Garden of England' for its gentle countryside, fruit trees and hops, but these are not the only things to flourish here. Cricket was already flourishing in Kent in the eighteenth century, although when the county took on England in 1799 they were soundly defeated. The following year they modestly fielded twenty-three men against England's twelve in a return match. In 1847, however, the county played All England in a proper eleven-a-side match and won a pulsating game by one wicket! Several of Kent's finest cricketers are also counted amongst the game's great eccentrics. One of the earliest was Alfred Mynn,

whose twenty-stone bulk did not prevent him being a great all-rounder: fast bowler, clean hitter and slip fielder with magnetic hands. Of the same era were Fuller Pilch, who perfected the art of playing forward, and Nicholas Wanostrocht, perpetual joker on and off the field, who played under the alias of 'Felix' so as not to damage his reputation as a headmaster. In *Felix on the Bat* (1845), Wanostrocht wrote the first scientific treatise on batting. Later Kentish heroes are as memorable for the way they played the game as for the

records they achieved. Frank Woolley, the ultimate in left-handed style and grace, not only scored sixty thousand runs in his first-class career, but also took over two thousand wickets. A.P. 'Titch' Freeman, purveyor of buzzing leg breaks and googlies, took 3,775 wickets in all, including 304 in 1928. D.V.P. Wright delivered his leg breaks and googlies at a fast-medium pace to such effect that he did the hat-trick seven times in his career. Then there are the Kentish wicket-keepers, of whom none was ever sounder than

In the 'garden of England' hops are not the only things to flourish. Cricket is alive and well on Kent's village greens.

L.E.G. Ames, who also scored eight test match centuries; none more effective than Alan Knott; none more brilliant than W.H.V. 'Hopper' Levett; and none more flamboyant than Godfrey Evans. In his day, Evans could turn a match with one diving catch, or inspire a bowler like Alec Bedser, whose fast, swinging cutters always made Evans stand up to the wicket.

The national passion for cricket has brought out the best in British prose writers, from E.V. Lucas, Siegfried Sassoon and Hugh de Selincourt to Neville Cardus, A.A. Thomson and Benny Green. The best cricket verse is usually of a jocular kind, as written by R.C. Robertson-Glasgow and Herbert Farjeon. True, some very good modern poets have written cricket verse, notably John Arlott, Edmund Blunden and Alan Ross, but this is of far less significance than their prose writings about the game. Blunden, who played in gym

Far left: a Kentish hop-field. Hops were mentioned by the Roman writer Pliny as a plant eaten like asparagus, but since the eighth century their primary use has been to give flavour to beer. They were introduced into England in 1525, since when Kent has been by far the country's biggest grower. Above: waiting to go in to bat is a tense time for cricketers, young and old. Windmills (left) and oast houses (far left) are traditional features of the Kentish landscape.

shoes and never wore batting gloves, was a devilishly difficult batsman to dismiss. He spent his early years in Kent, and in his book, *Cricket Country* (1943), he succeeded in evoking the essence of the game as it was, and still is, played at weekends on village greens and rural pitches throughout the English summer. For the players, however modest their record, there is always the possibility that today is the day on which they will bowl the unplayable ball, take the incredible catch or play the impeccable stroke.

Summer

BIGGIN HILL INTERNATIONAL AIR FAIR

The first powered and controlled flight by a heavier-than-air machine is said to have been that of Orville Wright in the USA in 1903, when he flew a distance of 852 feet. However, the romance and glamour associated with flying only began with the aces of World War I. On 1 April 1915, a French officer of the Aviation Militaire, Roland Garros, engaged and shot down a surprised German reconnaissance aircraft. Up until then, combatants had engaged each other in the air with rifle and revolver fire, breaking away with a gentlemanly wave of the hand when, as was usually the

case, these tactics brought no perceptible success. What Roland Garros did was as conclusive as it was revolutionary. He arranged to have a machine gun mounted on the fuselage of his monoplane, so that he could fire along the line of his flight through the propeller blades. Thus began the era of aerial acrobatics and tactics. Soon men of the Royal Flying Corps, which became the Royal Air Force in 1918, and of the German Jagdstaffeln were matching each other in the

skies and individual dog-fights gave way to sophisticated swirlings of whole squadrons in combat with each other. The immediate successors to this tradition were the men and planes who fought in World War II. Then the incomparable Spitfires and Hurricanes clashed with Messerschmitts, and the names of men like 'Ginger' Lacey and 'Sailor' Malan, Adolf Galland and Werner Mölders, joined those of the flying aces immortalised in World War I. Their modern counterparts

Top left: one of the Red Arrows gets ready for takeoff, whilst stunt planes of an earlier age (top right) line up on the field. Above left: a Sopwith Pup shadowed by a Harrier GR5. Above: Squadron Leader Doug Gregory with his DIY SE5a.

are the pilots of air forces throughout the world, flying Tornados, Harriers, Phantoms, Hawks, Thunderbolts and the like. Once a year, at Biggin Hill Airport in Kent, machines covering the whole era of aeronautics and their pilots are brought together for an exhibition of aircraft and a fiesta of flying. It is an annual mecca for the enthusiast where, despite the glamour that is inevitably associated with the triumphs of modern technology, the achievements and abilities of classic aircraft are also remembered and savoured. World War II bombers like the Shackleton, the Flying Fortress and the Lancaster, and the Catalina flying boat all have their place in the flying parade. As does that modern work-horse, the helicopter, under various names such as Alouette, Sioux, Skeeter and Lynx. Those intrepid men who form the country's various parachute display teams also have a part to play, as does British Airways'

A replica Red Baron Fokker Triplane from World War I (left) shares the stage with a Douglas C47 (below), a De Havilland Canada CC-142 Dash-8 passenger/cargo transport plane (below centre) and a Royal Navy Sea Fury (bottom).

Concorde, which wings its way majestically over the fair. More unusual exhibits may well include an aerobatic gliding team, a 'girl on a wing', and a hot-air balloon, while the real connoisseur of the bizarre may catch sight of three Frenchmen actually carrying their aeroplanes to the starting line. These are the pilots of the incredible Cri-Cris, or Crickets. Although no larger than some model planes, they are powered by two fifteen-horse-power, two-stroke engines and not only

People are as much a feature of the show as planes. Pilots of aircraft ancient and modern together with daredevil stunt artists perform before an enthusiastic audience.

ROYAL AIR FORCE

fly, but perform aerobatics, too.

Nostalgia forms a large part of the fair's appeal to the aeroplane enthusiast. It is one thing to possess pictures or models of the great originals like the SE5a and the Red Baron Fokker Triplane, or to be able to examine them under museum conditions, but it is quite another experience to watch them in the air, recreating the combat manoeuvres of World War I, and to be able to take one's own photographs of the action from a grandstand view. A mock battle between a Spitfire and a Messerschmitt provides an opportunity to see the various tactics used in World War II, whilst a totally different war situation is recalled as a Japanese Zero fighter attacks an American Beech C45 Expeditor support aircraft. To demonstrate pure aerobatics, there are not only the phenomenal Red Arrows in their glossy red Hawks, but also the Airtour Diamond Nine, a squadron of Tiger Moth biplanes. As the Red Arrows perform their breathtaking aerial manoeuvres, which call for absolute precision and timing and supreme flying skill, it is salutary to remember that these pilots are not circus performers, but serving Royal Air Force officers, whose planes, in time of crisis, would simply need to be repainted and armed in order to take their place as part of Britain's air defence forces.

Summer

SUMMER IN THE CITY

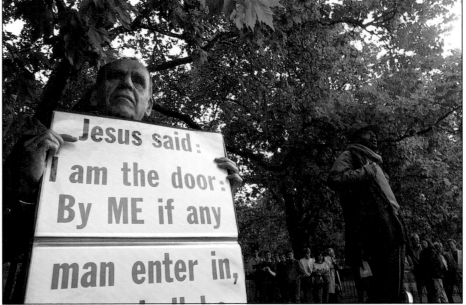

When Wordsworth composed the lines, 'Earth hath not anything to show more fair: / Dull would he be of soul who could pass by, / A sight so touching in its majesty', he was recalling the deep feelings inspired by the view from Westminster Bridge across the sweep of the River Thames towards the City of London. No river in the world is more steeped in history. It rises near Cirencester in the Cotswolds and follows a course of 190 miles until it reaches the sea near Gravesend. Once, it was even longer, and in the distant past may have continued across an enormous plain, now the North Sea, to join the Rhine and the Elbe and debouch into the Norwegian seas. The present-day Thames

snakes through Oxford and passes the playing fields of Eton, taking in Henley, Reading, and royal Windsor, before flowing on through Hampton Court, Richmond, Mortlake, Hammersmith and Putney and becoming, around Chelsea, the age-old highway of London itself. It was the river that gave London its name, for the Romans called their original settlement Londinium, or 'river place'. Kings and queens, prelates, statesmen and even traitors have been borne along the Thames.

At one time it carried the annual Lord Mayor's procession in a fleet of richly decorated barges along a route still travelled today by river-boats and launches, crowded with tourists. Until it was banked up on either side in the nineteenth century, the river was liable to freeze to a depth of several feet in severe winters, when ice fairs were held and oxen roasted over fires lit on the river's surface.

In 1179 the London Bridge that had been rebuilt

The modern builders of London (facing page) are always at work, changing the city's many faces (top left and top right). Centre: free speech at Speakers' Corner, Hyde Park, and the policemen (above) who maintain that freedom. Above left: summer solace outside a city pub.

Lake Havasu City, Arizona. The present bridge was then built on the site. Past London Bridge lies the Pool of London, crossed by Tower Bridge, beside which looms the Tower of London itself, built by William the Conqueror just outside the city walls to deter the citizens from doing anything rash. The old docks of London, which once served not only the whole of Britain but Europe too, are largely silent now, and in

Left: a traditional sailing barge becalmed in front of a modern Thamesside development, and (below) old Thames warehouses, decaying but still colourful.

on several occasions since Saxon times was replaced by a bridge of stone, 905 feet long and supported on nineteen great piers. It carried shops, apartments and even a chapel, as well as an array of spikes on which the heads of traitors were impaled. It has been said that the nursery rhyme, 'London Bridge is broken down', emanates from this period but, though it is of ancient origin, its composition has been traced no further back than the early seventeenth century. Until 1749, that bridge was the only one over the river in London, and it survived until 1831. Its replacement was 'broken down' in 1973 and transported, stone by stone, to

their place are modern developments such as St Katherine's Dock and Docklands, new centre of London's newspaper industry. At Greenwich, though, the old glory still survives in Sir Christopher Wren's triumphant architectural feat, the Royal Hospital for Seamen, renamed the Royal Naval College in 1873. The Thames continues past Woolwich, site until 1963 of the Royal Arsenal, through industrial wastelands and new town developments, and out to Erith and the Aveley Marshes, where the bones of a mammoth have been found. Finally, between Tilbury and Gravesend, the Thames flows out past Canvey Island to the sea.

Above: the Thames flood barrier at Woolwich, which weighs over three thousand tons and comprises vast steel gates that can rise from the river bed in thirty minutes when floodwaters threaten. Facing page: London's human and bird populations meet in the park.

Summer

STONEHENGE SUMMER SOLSTICE

Stonehenge is both the most dramatic and the most mysterious of all ancient British monuments. None of the other 900 stone circles which have been found throughout Europe can match it for the height of its stones and the precision with which they were positioned and shaped. It is also unique in that it had, and in some cases still has, huge stone lintels balanced across its uprights. Stonehenge was built in four stages, beginning in about 2200 B.C. with a simple earthwork. The construction of the great stone circle,

with an avenue extending to the river Avon, spanned 1,000 years, beginning between 1700 and 1600 B.C. Stonehenge clearly had some religious significance, possibly connected with the relative positions of astronomical bodies at specific times. Certainly, on Midsummer Day, the sun does appear to rise over a point which corresponds to an axis of symmetry of the circle. On the basis that any pre-Christian religious rites in Britain must somehow be connected with the druids, the present-day Order of Druids has taken this site, and the ocasion of the summer solstice, as its own. However, the evidence is that the building and use of the circle predates the druids by many centuries.

The mystic moment of sunrise (above) on Midsummer day draws the modern Druids to Stonehenge. They come to celebrate the solstice, bearing what they believe to be the ancient symbols of their calling (top and far left). The ceremony (facing page bottom) is apparently attended by as many photographers as Druids. In recent years it has also been invaded by hippies (left), who are now banned from coming anywhere near the site. Facing page top right: hippies occupy the Heel Stone, which is one of the oldest of the pillars and which once stood upright. Facing page top left: the modern face of Druidism.

Summer

ROYAL ASCOT RACES

Her Majesty the Queen, in addition to possessing a palace in London, castles at Windsor and Balmoral, a holiday home at Sandringham and twelve parks in the London area, is also the owner of a racecourse, Ascot, situated conveniently near Windsor Castle. The annual June meeting is called Royal Ascot and is the premier event in the British racing calendar. People come to this meeting to see and be seen, so it is an occasion of typically British pomp and elegance, when top hats are taken out and dusted, morning suits hired, and the prettiest and most fashionable of summer dresses acquired. Traditionally, each day begins with HM the Queen and other members of the royal family riding

Hats, and the outfits that go with them, are a very important part of Royal Ascot, but the racing is worth seeing, too! The men may not be able to achieve much variety with their top hats, but for the women it's the year's great opportunity to go to town with their headgear. The results range from the conventionally pretty to the unusual and even the downright bizarre. As the carriage of HM the Queen (left) passes the Queen Elizabeth Stand, the military band strikes up the National Anthem.

from Windsor Castle along the course. Their carriages are drawn by pairs of horses from the royal stables with mounted grooms in full livery, and coachmen in black and gold top hats and red coats with gold buttons. Royal Ascot is also a field day for the upholders of protocol. Less than a generation ago, no divorced person was allowed into the royal enclosure, a throwback to Victorian views on the sanctity of marriage and family life. When George V allowed the 'innocent parties' of divorces to attend Royal Ascot, it was

regarded as the quintessence of progressiveness. On the question of female dress, trouser suits have been banned since 1967, when the Duke of Norfolk, the arbiter in such matters, forbade them to be worn. He did not, however, pronounce on hemlines, so the variety of hemlines is as astonishing as that of the dresses in general. All kinds of hats, too, are as confidently worn as they are universally admired.

Ascot really began with Queen Anne, who had been introduced to horse racing as a teenager whilst

staying with her uncle, Charles II, and her father, the future James II, at Newmarket. In 1705, now Queen of England and Scotland and married to Prince George of Denmark, Anne made a royal progress to Newmarket, ordered the royal house there to be rebuilt, and paid a thousand guineas for a racehorse, which she presented to her husband. Then she watched the races. Whilst she was staying at Windsor Castle in 1711, she commanded that a race meeting should be organised on Ascot Common for her personal amusement, and drove there with her entourage, thus inaugurating the present tradition. It was, however, the first member of the royal family to be elected to the Jockey Club who put Ascot on the map as a prominent

racecourse. This was William Augustus, Duke of Cumberland, the second surviving son of George II. After the treaty of Aix-la-Chapelle which ended the War of the Austrian Succession and led to the reduction of the Britsh forces, he lived chiefly at Windsor in one or other of the royal lodges, greatly improving the park and founding the main Ascot race meeting. He was also the owner and breeder of both Herod and Eclipse, two of the greatest racehorses in the history of the sport. The Jockey Club still possesses a rather macabre trophy: one of Eclipse's hoofs, mounted on a golden salver and presented to the club by William IV, a great-nephew of William Augustus. At Ascot in 1791, another great-nephew, George, Prince of Wales won

Top left: formal dress is the order of the day for race officials, too. Entertainment is lavish whether it's a shady alfresco lunch (above left) or champagne to refresh the race-weary (left).

the Oatlands, a two-mile race, on his horse Baronet. In 1825, as George IV, he made the first official processional drive from Windsor Castle to Ascot racecourse. In 1829, from a new royal stand with an enclosure where he could entertain his friends, he saw not only one of the finest races ever run at Ascot, for that year's Gold Cup, but also what was regarded at the time as 'the grandest day ever seen at Ascot, both as to number of people, elegance of dress, and rank in life'. On such occasions and descriptions is tradition founded.

The Gold Cup was instituted in 1807 to mark the presence at the races of Queen Charlotte, wife of George III. William IV had the course refurbished and,

Amongst the elegant crowds there are apparently many serious race-goers, since over one million pounds is placed on each Royal Ascot race. Left and far left: a pink rose brightens a traditional outfit, whilst fabric flowers decorate a far from traditional one.

Colourful hats, luxurious Rolls Royces, well-chilled champagne, and long queues outside the Ladies – they're all an integral part of a day out at Royal Ascot. As are the horses, of course.

in 1838, the young Queen Victoria made the royal drive, wearing her ceremonial star and sash of honour, a pink dress and a white bonnet overlaid with pink ribbons and roses. It was her son, later Edward VII, who wrote to her of Royal Ascot: 'It is an opportunity for the Royal Family to show themselves in public – which I am sure you desire – and after all Racing with all its faults still remains, I may say, a National Institution of the Country.' Edward was himself a notable racehorse owner, whose Persimmon won the Derby and the St Leger in 1896, and was so hotly tipped to win the Ascot Gold Cup the following year that Queen Victoria,

who had not visited Ascot or any other racecourse since the death of her husband, Prince Albert, in 1861, was prevailed upon to come and watch the race. In the end, she was either delayed on her way from Balmoral, or could not face the public exposure, although the horse still won without her. Her successors, however, have remained loyal to Royal Ascot and have seen many exciting days' racing there. In 1972, Joe Mercer won the Prince of Wales Stakes on Brigadier Gerard, only a few days after rescuing three fellow-passengers from a plane crash. There was a stewards' enquiry after the Queen Anne Stakes in 1974, as a result of which the first three horses past the post were all disqualified, the second of them being Gloss, bred by HM the Queen herself. In the first running of the King George VI and Queen Elizabeth Diamond Stakes in 1975, Bustino and Grundy fought out the last furlong neck and neck for a photo finish, which placed Grundy fractionally ahead. Such incidents have made Royal Ascot memorable, though pride of place goes to its royal patrons and their loyal subjects, whose elegance on this ocasion lends it additional style.

Facing page: the ultimate in automotive one-upmanship: a vintage Rolls Royce.

Summer

A COTSWOLD LANDSCAPE

The Cotswold Hills, properly speaking, comprise a low limestone escarpment about fifty miles long, which rises up steeply on its western side and slopes down gently towards Oxford on its eastern side. That rather exclusive region known as the Cotswolds, however, comprises much of Gloucestershire and parts of adjoining counties, particularly Oxfordshire. It is a land of sheep, barley and the limestone itself, from which the houses are built. The stone is either golden or warm grey coloured and reflects the light, subtly changing tone with the weather to match the mood of the day. The stone's technical name is oolite, meaning egg stone, so called because its rounded grains are packed together like fish roe. As freestone it can readily be cut or carved, but it hardens with exposure to the elements. Where the limestone occurs in thin layers, these can be split to make the distinctive stone tiles with which many local houses are roofed. The Cotswold quarries, especially those situated around Burford, Taynton and the Barringtons, were already being excavated over 900 years ago. Most of the

Oxford colleges were built of Cotswold freestone, as was nearby Blenheim Palace and the interior of London's St Paul's Cathedral. The architect of Blenheim was Sir John Vanbrugh (1664-1726), comptroller of the queen's works and also author of two of the funniest Restoration comedies, The Relapse and The Provok'd Wife. When the Duke of Marlborough, for whom Blenheim Palace was being built at government expense, was sacked from all his posts in 1711, many of the costs already incurred devolved upon the unfortunate architect. Vanbrugh's official superior at this time was the aging Sir Christopher Wren (1632-

1723). In 1675, when Wren had begun to rebuild St Paul's after the Great Fire of London in 1666, he chose a Burford man as his clerk of works and Thomas Strong of Taynton as his master mason. Barges carrying the Cotswold limestone could easily be floated down the Windrush into the Thames and so to London.

The charm of the Cotswolds has not always been recognised. The political journalist William Cobbett (1763-1835) rode around southern England in 1822 to observe agricultural conditions. Of his first view of the Cotswolds, he wrote: 'I came up hill into a country, apparently formerly a down or common, but now

Facing page: 'Rose Cottage', but not a rose in sight on a Chipping Campden facade. Roofs, from the splendid in Chipping Campden (top left) to the quaint in Castle Combe (above), are often of local limestone, although the thatched cottage is also to be found (centre). Even the guard dog (top right) may be limestone and the garden wall (above left) almost certainly will be.

divided into large fields by stone walls. Anything so ugly I have never seen before.'

The Cotswolds' cult really began in 1871, when the poet and craftsman William Morris (1834-96) and his eccentric friend Dante Gabriel Rossetti (1828-82), both leading lights of the Pre-Raphaelite movement, became cotenants of Kelmscott Manor, situated on the border between Oxfordshire and Gloucestershire. One of Morris's interests was conservation and it was in the Cotswold village of Broadway that he wrote the letter that was instrumental in establishing the Society for the Protection of Ancient Buildings. Rossetti, meanwhile, was more interested in Morris's wife Jane, with whom he was hopelessly in love and whom he often used as a model for his paintings. Other artists followed Morris and Rossetti to the Cotswolds, including the American Edwin Abbey (1852-1911), who had settled in England in 1878. It was probably another American, the novelist Henry James (1843-1916), who, for better or worse, made the Cotswolds a fashionable residential area. In an article in Harper's

Bibury (top) competes with Castle Combe for the title of 'most beautiful village in England'. Limestone roof tiles are carefully graduated, with the heaviest hung at the bottom. Huge oak beams are required to support the weight of the roof. Picture-book cottages in Chipping Campden (left and far left) are almost clichés of the rural English dream. The luxuriant growth of the cottage garden is one happy result of the native climate. At a gymkhana in Long Compton (above), a nimble mount may make up for the lack of proportion between it and its rider .

Magazine he wrote: 'The place has so much character that it rubs off on the visitor, and if in an old garden with old gates and old walls, and old summer-houses, he lies down on the grass it is ten to one he will be converted. It is delicious to be at Broadway.' Edwin Abbey commented wryly that the article 'did not much help the privacy of the place'. Americans in particular, perhaps intrigued by the implications of the name, have been flocking to Broadway ever since. There actually once was an American actress on the Cotswold Broadway. In the 1890s, noted Shakespearean actress Mary Anderson (1863-1942) settled in the village with her husband. A few miles away, in Chipping Campden, there was an influx of a different kind. In 1888 Charles Ashbee (1863-1942), influenced by both the work and socialist principles of William Morris, had established the Guild of Handicraft in London. The Guild comprised a community of craftsmen whom Ashbee trained in furniture making, metalwork, jewellery making,

silversmithing, printing, and bookbinding 'in such a way as shall best conduce to the welfare of the workman'. In 1902 he transferred the 150-strong community of men, women and children to Chipping Campden. The Guild was wound up five years later, but not before Ashbee had restored a number of houses in the town's main street. Chipping Campden gained a more permanent champion with the formation in 1929 of the Campden Trust by Frederick Griggs (1876-1938), artist and engraver, who had lived there for many years. 'Chipping' means 'market' and, during the thirteenth and fourteenth centuries, the town was an important wool trade centre. It then fell into a commercial and industrial decline in spite of aid from the philanthropist Sir Baptist Hicks (1551-1629), who became Viscount Campden in 1628. Chipping Campden's almshouses, a fine example of Jacobean architecture, were built at his expense in 1612, and in 1627 he had the town's gabled market hall built with an open cobbled floor at ground level. His own great mansion, Campden House, was destroyed in the Civil War, but its curved gateway and lodges have survived. Sir Baptist and his wife lie in a special chapel in the fifteenth-century Church of St James, watched over by effigies of their daughter and son-in-law.

There are two contenders in the Cotswolds for the title of 'most beautiful village in England'. Bibury in Gloucestershire was the choice of William Morris. More recently the prize has gone to Castle Combe in Wiltshire. Bibury is situated by the River Coln. The bridge built over the river in 1777 is still in use. The church is mainly Anglo-Saxon and the churchyard contains several examples of a Cotswold speciality,

Manicured lawns and neat bedding plants lead the visitor up to the door of a typical Cotswold manor house in Chipping Campden (below far left). The patience of the angler (left) is legendary. Refreshment for a young gymkhana entrant (below) takes the heat out of the moment.

the 'bale tomb', which has a curved top like a tin loaf. Castle Combe lies in a valley, with cottages packed tightly on either side of a main street that runs down to a river. The church is an outstanding example of Early English Gothic and Perpendicular architecture.

The conservationists' successful battle to preserve the Cotswolds much as William Morris knew them has altered the area's social structure. Broken-down houses are being converted into picturesque cottages and sold

for vast sums as weekend or retirement homes for the well-heeled. More than thirty per cent of Chipping Campden's population is over sixty-five and only eight per cent of the pupils at its secondary school live in the town itself. A hundred years ago, Chipping Campden's farmworkers provided agricultural labour for the whole district. Today, they can no longer afford to buy the cottages which were originally built for them and workers have to be bussed in daily from Birmingham.

A great British pastime – coarse fishing in the rain. Ranged along the banks of the river Windrush near Burford, true anglers do not allow the weather to dampen their enthusiasm.

Summer

WIMBLEDON, THE WAITING GAME

As one American visitor is reported to have remarked: 'There may not always be an England but, by God, sir, there will always be a Wimbledon.' The mystique of the Wimbledon Tennis Championships, which take place over a fortnight at the end of June, does not just lie in the fact that it was the first event of its kind, the men's championship beginning in 1877, the ladies' singles and men's doubles in 1884, nor in that it is the only grand slam event still to be played on grass; nor in that the royal box is usually occupied by at least one

member of the royal family together with other notables; nor in that it brings together all the greatest players in the world. None of these factors alone is sufficient to explain Wimbledon fever, which causes people willingly to suffer many privations simply to get into the ground and then, in many cases, considerable further discomfort once they are inside. Queuing patiently has long been a British custom, but one to which foreigners have never taken – except, it would seem, during Wimbledon fortnight. At the head of the queue, which snakes back

for miles from the gates, will be those stalwarts who have been there all night. If the unpredictable British weather does not stop play, they will be rewarded with a prime position from which to watch the match of their choice, provided they run fast enough once they have been let through the gates. Those much farther down the queue might be lucky to get a few hours' standing in the open watching the players perform.

The Wimbledon championships are not only an oligarchic institution, but also, in sporting terms, a

'If you can wait and not be tired by waiting ...' Rudyard Kipling's words never seem more appropriate than when applied to those who wait hopefully for tickets or custom during Wimbledon fortnight.

positively anachronistic one. The event is organised and run by the somewhat inappropriately named All England Lawn Tennis and Croquet Club, a private club with only 375 members. The championships employ almost 3,000 people, over 1,000 of whom are involved on the catering side. The smooth running of the matches themselves is in the hands of 358 court officials and 120 ball boys and girls, who are recruited from local schools. Cool nerves, sound judgment, and split-second timing are required to organise the playing of 443 main championship matches and 357 other matches on the eighteen courts. A careful balance must be maintained between giving spectators on the two main courts the chance to see what are expected to be the day's best matches and allowing as many of the top players as possible to experience the conditions on these courts. Rain can demolish the best-laid plans.

On one awful occasion in 1985 a flash storm hit the ground, flooded it and blew out the computer.

Playing at Wimbledon has a cachet all of its own. Being a spectator is equally special. It is not just the players nor the strawberries and cream that give Wimbledon its particular appeal. The conviviality of the event and the intimacy of the surroundings create a special atmosphere which heightens the excitement and increases the sensation, as you surge round in the crowds, of participating in a unique occasion.

Wimbledon inspires people to search out their rackets, and the area suddenly abounds with tennis players (top). Left: a dispiriting message broadcast by sandwich-board. Everybody is alive to the commercial opportunities of Wimbledon, and T-shirts are for sale even in suburban streets (above).

Summer

TT RACING, ISLE OF MAN

The Isle of Man is British yet not, strictly speaking, a part of Britain. It is a Crown possession, with its own parliament and legal system, but dependent on the British Government in matters of defence and international relations. It is a member of the European Economic Community for customs' purposes and in respect of certain aspects of the Common Agricultural Policy, but it pays no contributions to the Community, nor receives any funds from it. Its name derives from the Manx words 'ellan vannin' meaning 'island in the middle', an accurate description of this small island situated in the middle of the Irish Sea between England

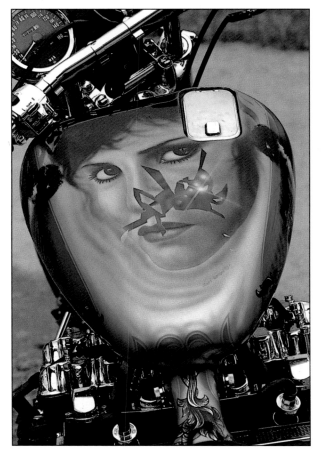

Traditional fishing boats (top right) and even the Red Arrows display team (above far left) take second place to motorcycles ancient and modern at the TT races. Eccentricity of dress amongst racing enthusiasts includes Viking-style horns on an old helmet (facing page), yet even the macho leather-clad enjoy an ice cream (above centre).

and Ireland. It was part of the Norwegian kingdom until 1266, when it was ceded to Alexander III of Scotland. In 1406 it came into the hands of the Earls of Derby and then passed to the Dukes of Atholl, from whom it was purchased by the British Government in 1765 after protracted negotiations. The island's parliament, the Tynwald, was founded by the Vikings and has two branches, the Legislative Council and the House of Keys.

June brings hordes of motorcycle enthusiasts to the island for the annual Tourist Trophy races. These have been in existence for almost as long as the motorcycle itself. The development of the latter was dependent on various inventions, beginning with that of a four-stroke engine in Germany in 1876. This used a piston and valves to drive a crankshaft or wheel and was similar to the type usually used today for machines with an engine capacity of 250cc and upwards. In 1885, Gottleib Daimler attached a petrol engine to a bicycle and in 1887 Felix Millet built a multicylinder motorcycle. A pneumatic tyre had been patented in 1845 by a Scottish engineer, Robert Thomson, who did not proceed with its production because of the high cost of rubber. When another Scot, a veterinary surgeon called John Boyd Dunlop, reinvented the device in 1888, it made his fortune. Excelsior built the first British motorcycle in 1896. The following year the

Horseless Vehicle Journal reported on a race between a motorcycle and a bicycle – the bicycle won by 300 yards! A design with the engine low down between the wheels was promoted in France in 1901 and in 1903 Harley Davidson in the USA and Triumph in Britain began to manufacture motorcycles commercially.

Early races were held at Canning Town, Crystal Palace and Herne Hill and in 1903 Harry Martin, on an Excelsior machine, covered a mile in one minute twenty-four seconds from a standing start. An annual International Cup race, between Austria, Britain, Denmark, France and Germany, was instituted in 1904. The first Tourist Trophy race in the Isle of Man was held in 1907. It was won by Charlie Collier, one of two racing sons of the founder of the Matchless company, who covered the 158-mile course in four hours eight minutes and eight seconds, an average speed of 38.22 mph. It was an historic occasion.

The organisers of the British team for the

The races require great concentration from participants and spectators alike. Relaxing in the sun or attending a wet T-shirt competition in a local night-club relieves the tension.

International Cup race in 1905 had held their trials in the Isle of Man, where English regulations imposing strict speed limits and forbidding the closing of roads for racing did not apply. The Auto-Cycle Club, founded in 1903, now approached the Isle of Man Government about holding a regular series of road races on the island. Their response was enthusiastic. By the 1920s the legendary mountain course had been mapped out, providing men and their machines with a yardstick against which to measure and develop their feats of endurance and engineering. In 1923 both the junior, or lightweight, and senior races were held over six laps, a distance of 226.5 miles. The junior was won at an average speed of 55.73 mph. By 1932 the winner's average speed had advanced to 77.16 mph. One of the most sensational races ever took place in 1935. Jimmy Guthrie crossed the line with a lead of twenty-six seconds over Stanley Woods, who still had a lap to

mph from a standing start. At this time no one could contemplate world championship motorcycle racing without the Isle of Man TT races. Yet, in 1976, the meeting ceased to be one of the events on the grand prix circuit because of criticism from top riders and concern that the invention of faster, heavier and more sophisticated machines had resulted in an increasing number of accidents, many of them fatal, on a course whose lap of thirty-seven miles was difficult to get to know well and whose eccentricities might be forgotten in the heat of a race. The races themselves are still held, over the same course, and the event brings some 30,000 people and 10,000 motorbikes to the island every year. The meeting may have lost its grand prix status, but its attraction persists. It was certainly as exciting as ever in 1979 when, twenty years after he had first ridden the course, Mike Hailwood returned for the senior event, which he won on a 500cc Suzuki,

Despite the shattering noise of the motorcycles and the reputations often attributed to their riders, those that come to the Isle of Man for the TT races are warmly welcomed and splendidly behaved. For hotels (below and below left) at least, the TT races provide a good source of income.

go. Woods had not refuelled his machine at the halfway stage, as was the usual practice, and he seemed bound to take a pit-stop now. Instead Woods decided to go for broke. He ignored his pit crew as they stood with their fuel nozzles at the ready and pushed his machine beyond its safe limits. He won by four seconds, having covered the last lap at a record 86.53 mph. The first Japanese machines made their debut on the mountain course in 1959 and the matchless Mike Hailwood won a record three races in a week in 1961, riding a Honda. In 1968 Bill Ivy, riding a 125cc Yamaha, became the first rider ever to cover a lap of the course at an average speed of over 100 mph when, in the 250cc race, he achieved a lap speed of 105.51

The assembled ranks of motorcycles are as great a spectator sport as the races themselves.

thus completing a record number of fourteen wins in the Isle of Man TT races.

The controversy about the course has intensified in recent years. Early in the 1989 meeting the lap record was broken by a Manxman, Phil Hogg. By the halfway point of the second week, he was one of no less than five riders, two of them of world renown, who had been killed on different sections of the same 1,300cc race. The irony of Hogg's record was that it was broken twice before the end of the meeting, first by another Manxman and then by a Scot, John Hislop, who also broke the race record. Hislop was the first rider ever to complete a lap in under nineteen minutes and only the third, after Hailwood and Joey Dunlop,

The fortnight's programme offers forty races for nine motorcycle categories, plus over 2,000 miles of practice laps (below, below centre and bottom). Below far left: not all spectators are leather clad. Left: the front at Douglas, beneath the island's flag. English machines (centre left) are few and far between and often vintage. Facing page: local and TT atmosphere on the Isle of Man.

to register three wins in one Isle of Man TT meeting. He achieved this after miraculously surviving a 140 mph crash! It is not difficult to argue that the Isle of Man TT races should be abandoned completely. Since 1907, 151 riders have lost their lives on the course, more than one fatality per meeting. An alternative might be to review the course itself, sacrosanct since the 1920s, and iron out the hazards. In defence of the TT races, it is said that banning them entirely would severely damage the Isle of Man's economy, whilst changing the course would destroy both its mystique and its challenge. It seems that, for the time being anyway, tradition and demand will prevail. Most of the riders who come to race in the Isle of Man in June pay to do so. At a second meeting, in August, the races are open to amateurs and no prize money is offered. Death on the roads, in the air or even on the railways has become an everyday hazard. Those who risk their lives practising dangerous sports do so not for the money, for amateurs there is none, but for the sheer personal satisfaction of rising to the physical and mental challenge.

Summer

A ROYAL GARDEN PARTY

The invitation, embossed in gold with a crown and the Queen's monogram, comes from the Lord Chamberlain's Office. The Lord Chamberlain 'is commanded by Her Majesty' to invite the recipient to 'an Afternoon Party'. 'Morning Dress or Uniform or Lounge Suit' is stipulated. It is expected that those invited will attend, so people are asked to reply only if they are unable to go. The pattern is the same, whether the party is in the gardens of London's Buckingham Palace or those of Edinburgh's Palace of Holyrood House, which the royal family usually visits each summer. At precisely the appointed hour, Her Majesty emerges from the palace together with other members of the royal family. A few carefully chosen guests will be shepherded into position to be presented to the Queen and exchange a few words with her or with one of her entourage. For other guests, it is a case of extricating something to eat and drink from one of several marquees or of finding a vantage point from which to gape at the royals. The rest wander round the gardens themselves or simply sit and drink in the curiously archaic atmosphere of the occasion.

Lining up is an integral part of a royal garden party. An array of toppers (top left) and a clutch of clerics, including the Archbishop of Canterbury and Archbishop Desmond Tutu (top right) watch and wait. The lines move and reform around the privileged few who are being presented to the royals (left). Summer hats may be worn by female guests but the wise carry an umbrella too. Facing page: gentleman-in-waiting.

When the present queen acceded to the throne, she was sitting in a tree in a game reserve in Kenya. She was not quite twenty-six and the mother of two very young children. Her father, George VI, had died unexpectedly from a coronary thrombosis during the night of 6 February 1952. Elizabeth II then became not only queen of Great Britain and Northern Ireland and head of the Commonwealth, but also head of state of seventeen members of the Commonwealth, ranging in size from Canada and Australia to St Kitts, Nevis and Tuvalu. She is Supreme Commander of the British Armed Forces, Head of the Church of England and the source of justice. The government act in her name and on her behalf. The prime minister and members of the cabinet are her servants and, constitutionally, require

Colour and tradition are the order of the day. The Beefeaters (below far left) fulfil both criteria with great flair. Archbishops and bishops also lend colour to the scene (left). Tradition prevails in this badge of office worn by one guest (below).

HRH the Princess of Wales (left) does her garden party piece with all her usual style and grace. Above: sartorial elegance, with umbrella. Facing page top left: HM the Queen in conversation. Facing page bottom left: 'Present mirth hath present laughter' (Shakespeare, Twelfth Night, 3, 1). Royal watching, whether professionally (facing page top right) or as an amateur (facing page bottom right) is the focal point of every garden party.

her consent for their every decision. In addition, she is Colonel in Chief of a formidable battery of army regiments in Britain and the Commonwealth, Air Commodore in Chief of the Australian Citizens Air Force, Hon. Commissioner of the Royal Canadian Mounted Police, Master of the Merchant Navy and Fishing Fleets and Head of the Civil Defence Corps. As far as the practicalities are concerned, her actual power is virtually nil and the government of the day will 'recommend' her to approve whatever their parliamentary party and the electorate will support. She may not publicly express a political opinion, nor,

officially, even have one. It is dignity, rather than emotion, that the queen is required to display. This petite woman, a mere five feet four inches tall, who may be seen formally dressed in coat and hat, informally dressed in wellington boots and headscarf or, on state occasions, wearing her crown together with spectacles and carrying a handbag, is simply a figurehead. But what a figurehead! For, though prime ministers and governments may come and go, the British monarchy, in the person of Her Majesty the Queen, provides a permanent source of inspiration and a focus of affection for the British people such as no republic can have.

Summer

THE WEST'S SUMMER SEASON

The historic village of Abbotsbury lies just inland from the Dorset coast by the lagoon formed behind the Chesil Bank. There has been a swannery on the lagoon since the fourteenth century but, apart from some interesting fragments of masonry, all that remains of the monastery that established this swannery is the vast tithe barn which stands proudly to the south of the mainly fifteenth- and sixteenth-century parish church. Bullet holes in the pulpit canopy testify to the ferocity with which the Civil War was fought thereabouts.

Further along the coast, in Devon, seaside resorts have grown up in the natural bays. These range from modern resorts, such as Seaton, to those of a more venerable kind, such as Sidmouth. Originally, Sidmouth was just a fishing village but when, between 1803 and 1815, the Napoleonic Wars put paid to continental holidays for leisured Britons, it became an exclusive resort. It even inspired a distinctive seaside form of Georgian architecture, featuring white, wrought-iron

Abbotsbury's main street (top pictures) boasts thatched roofs as a feature of its western end. Boats, on the beach at Sidmouth (above far left) or in Fowey harbour (far left), are always a favourite feature of the seaside. The cliffs at Seaton are a spectacular setting for a game of golf (above and left), whilst one of the joys of retirement is having all the time in the world to relax in a deckchair (above centre).

balconies. The row of terraced houses that comprises Fortfield Terrace, where the poet Elizabeth Barrett Browning lived with her father, brothers and sisters from 1832 to 1835, fronts Sidmouth's famous cricket ground, already in existence in Elizabeth's day.

The coast of Cornwall is altogether craggier, a difference befitting the fact that the Cornish have a culture and a language which, though Celtic based, are entirely their own. Fowey has been a seaport since at least the fourteenth century, when the notorious Fowey Gallants would sail out on pirate raids along the French coast. Newlyn is noted for both its fishing and

Above: the perils of historical quaintness embodied in a cardboard cut-out of Henry VIII which peers out of an Abbotsbury antiques and crafts shop. No doubt this is purely to tempt the tourists, for Henry VIII had no connection with the village, whose origins go back at least five hundred years before his time. Left and above left: two traditional Newlyn pursuits on the beach. The artists' colony which was centred on Newlyn during the nineteenth century moved on to St Ives many decades ago, but the fishing industry still flourishes.

its artists, but, though it is still one of the main centres for deep-sea fishing in Britain, the artists' colony is no more, though painters do still frequent the town.

The spectacular Cornish coast is notorious not only for its pirates and smugglers, but also for its mists and rocks. Close to Lizard Point, the southernmost tip of Britain, are buried 200 bodies found on the shore below on a single day in the mid-eighteenth century. The present lighthouse was built in 1752 and was given a more powerful lighting system at the beginning of this century. Its beam is said to have been seen a hundred miles out to sea.

The weather is not allowed to interfere with performances at the extraordinary Minack Theatre, right on the coast by Porthcurno and only a few miles from Land's End. This open-air venue was created in 1932 from a gorse-filled granite gully which sloped down to the sea. Audiences are advised to wear warm clothing, bring rugs and always telephone for an on-the-spot weather report before a visit. Porthcurno appears to have its own climatic conditions and, on average, less than three performances are cancelled in any season, which lasts from May to September.

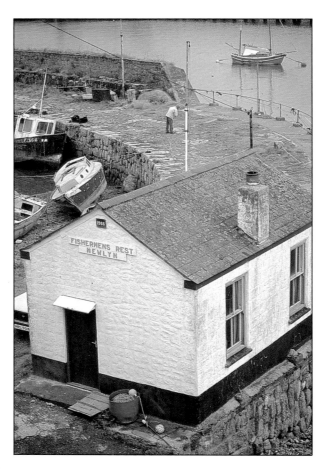

Top: cornish coastal mists wreathe the craggy coastline, whose southernmost tip is Lizard Point (above and above centre). Left: an aptly-named Newlyn haven. Above left and far left: 'Singing in the Rain' in the Cambridge University Gilbert and Sullivan Society's performance of HMS Pinafore at the Minack Theatre. Facing page: the church at Widecombe-in-the-Moor, Dartmoor, known as the 'cathedral of the moor'.

HENLEY ROYAL REGATTA

The River Thames, so bound up with English history on its course through London, has also inspired a quintessentially English event that takes place on the river as it passes through the pleasant town of Henley-on-Thames, some fifty miles or so up its meandering course. For sheer exclusivity it outdoes even Royal Ascot and the Wimbledon Tennis Championships.

The first Henley regatta was held in 1839 as a means of providing amusement and profit for the town and its people. Bell's Life and Chronicle reported that, at a public meeting held earlier that year to air the proposal, the chairman 'alluded to the lethargy which had so long prevailed on the subject of aquatics; and

said that at last so strong an interest had been manifested in the subject that, independent of the amusement to be derived from the establishment of a regatta, under judicious management it could not fail to be of great benefit to the town'. The regatta first achieved its royal status in 1851, when Albert, Prince Consort of Queen Victoria, became its patron. Since then the patron of the event has always been the reigning monarch. It was more than forty years after the first race before any rowing man was called on to assist in the actual

organisation of the event. Nevertheless, the Henley Royal Regatta came to have a profound influence on the course of rowing as an amateur sport both in Britain and internationally. The regatta's organisation is still in the hands of an unlimited number of self-appointed stewards, who elect from amongst themselves a committee of not more than twelve 'to exercise control over all matters connected with the regatta'. It is these stewards who have hitherto banned women from competing in the event and who have

Facing page: a close finish. Whilst spectators settle down to enjoy a picnic on the water (top right), crews experience the agony of pre-race tension. Top left: a coxed four, with almost submerged cox, rows up towards the start and (left) an eight prepares to go out. Above centre: boaters and refreshments for the boys of Bedford School, who are here to cheer on their crew. Above centre left: the all-important Stewards' Enclosure entrance badge hangs from the lapel of a club blazer. Pink caps and ties (above) are worn by the members of Leander, Britain's most prestigious rowing club, which is based in Henley.

issued ordinances regarding permitted female dress.

Since the inception of the event, the interests of spectators have been well catered for, even if the locals suffer some disruption to their lives as a result. On the day of the first regatta, according to a press report, 'at five o'clock a merry peal aroused the inhabitants and the busy din of preparation was heard in finishing the various erections by the waterside'. On the previous evening there had been a storm of such violence that 'the chimney of Mr Cooper's Assembly Rooms in Bell Street was struck by the electric fluid' and there was no improvement in the weather until the following

were washed down with a liberal supply of alcohol, without which, some cynical observers have suggested, the modern event would not survive: 'Take away the oarsmen and you would still have Henley; take away the booze and you wouldn't.' Female spectators have to undergo careful scrutiny as they enter the exclusive Stewards' Enclosure. Rule 6 of the stewards' regulations reads, at the time of writing, 'Ladies should wear dresses or suits and will not be admitted wearing skirts above the knee, divided skirts, culottes or trousers of any kind, shorts, jeans or denim suits.' Security guards checking entrance passes also ensure that Rule 6 is

Left: two eights begin the journey up to the start, tracked by some of the many pleasure craft that ply the river during the regatta. Behind them stretch the arches of Henley Bridge, built in 1786. Below: a moment of quiet contemplation. Bottom left: limbering up for the crews and (bottom centre) cooling down for spectators.

Henley is a traditional occasion when generations mingle (facing page), united in their enthusiasm for rowing. Many veteran rowers still proudly sport their club's colours (above).

afternoon. Even so, 'spectators to the amount of 9,000 or 10,000 assembled on the Bridge, and on either bank of the River, also in stands which had been erected for the purpose, or on barges in the water decorated with flags. The bells of the Parish Church were ringing the best portion of the day, and cannon fired at intervals, and two bands of music on the water playing popular airs alternately.' The refreshments that have become inseparable from the event were available then, too, and 'between the various heats, a number of gentlemen were invited to partake of excellent cold collations, at the residences of Messrs Brakespear, Nash, Hickman, Stubbs and other gentlemen of the Committee'. No doubt these collations

observed, acting as self-styled arbiters of fashion in doubtful cases.

Henley Royal Regatta lasts four days, during which are run the heats and finals of fourteen events, of which the Grand Challenge Cup, for eights, and the Diamond Sculls, for single oarsmen, are the most prestigious. The regatta is an international occasion, at which crews and oarsmen from the USA, USSR, Canada and Australia compete against those from Britain and other European countries. Normally, an international regatta race is rowed in six lanes along a featureless 2,000-metre course and includes a repechage heat, which gives those eliminated in earlier heats a second chance to qualify for the final. At one mile 550 yards, the Henley course is slightly longer. What makes Henley special, increasing the tension and spurring the oarsmen to give their utmost, is that there are only two lanes and each heat is sudden death. Daniel Topolski, who rowed in 75 races at Henley over 25 years, has summed up the agony and the ecstasy of the event: 'With lungs bursting and legs

burning, you reach the Enclosures with the shouts and cheers increasing to a roar as you approach the finishing line. Polite applause and sympathetic calls greet the victim of an 'easily' verdict. But the wall of noise that welcomes the combatants of a close-fought struggle, or a popular local winner, is an experience never forgotten. To snatch a victory in the dying seconds of a race provides the sweetest and most memorable bliss.'

Gold medals for British oarsmen at the last two Olympic Games, in Seoul and Los Angeles, have increased public interest in this wholly amateur sport and ensured the fullest of houses at each Henley Royal Regatta. The organisers see no need for the time being to alter the regatta itself nor the way in which it is run and even less need to sell out to a sponsor. In its present form Henley Royal Regatta is both the most prestigious event in the international rowing calendar and the last of the great English garden parties. Each individual, whether participant or spectator, can derive from the occasion maximum satisfaction on either front – if the notorious British weather cooperates.

Nautical blue and white stripes, spruce blazers and jaunty straw hats are favourite forms of dress on regatta days. Houses with river frontage (top) provide a welcome haven from the milling crowds in the official enclosures.

Summer

THE ROYAL WELSH SHOW

Given the Welsh flair for showmanship and the Welsh economy's reliance on agriculture and tourism, it is hardly surprising that these should find spectacular expression in the form of the annual Royal Welsh Show. A permanent national showground was established almost thirty years ago at Llanelwedd, Builth Wells, but the regions have not been forgotten in that, every year, a different county in the principality is specially featured. To say that the event is a rural extravaganza would be to undervalue the variety of spectacle and entertainment on offer over the four days of the show, preceded on the Sunday by a special service at St Mary's Church, Builth Wells and a Young Farmers' Club Grand Concert at the Strand Hall.

Top left and above: Welsh Cobs show their paces. The hardy native breeds will bear the weight of an adult male and make good working ponies (far left). Native breeds of sheep (top right) also feature prominently at the show, but in the cattle section (left) there are more classes for foreign breeds.

There are several venues, including the main ring, cattle ring, horse ring, sports arena, livestock area, forestry section, flower tent and the fur and feather building. The impression of the show as a veritable hive of activity is heightened by the rows of trade stands, stalls and pens containing horses, cattle, sheep, goats and pigs, by the continuous demonstrations of agricultural machinery and implements and by the appearances of brass and jazz bands. Throughout there is a judicious blend of traditional competition and unusual entertainment. Pride of place goes of course to the animals, most especially the Welsh breeds. Amongst the breeds of sheep to be judged are the Welsh Mountain, South Wales Mountain, Hill Radnor, Black Welsh Mountain, Welsh Hill Speckled Face, Brecknock Hill Type, Balwen Welsh Mountain and others, all specially bred for grazing and breeding in hilly country. There are also competitions for live lambs, dead lambs in carcass form and fleeces. Welsh cattle are less in evidence and only the Welsh Black and the neighbouring Hereford classes stand out amongst those for the British Charolais, Murray Grey Beef, Blond d'Aquitaine, Limousin, Simmental, Red Poll, Poll Charolais and British Belgian Blue. Amongst the many horse sections are those for Welsh cobs and Welsh mountain ponies, lively breeds evolved in harsh

Below far left: HRH the Prince of Wales chats with exhibitors in the cattle ring. On the third day, the open sheep dog trial (left), held outside the show's arena, provides some tense moments. Will the sheep go into the pen (bottom)? Below: expert judgment. When it comes to the horse judging, the Welsh Mountain pony's head (below centre) is paramount, as is the pace of the Welsh Cob (below centre left).

conditions. There are contests for sheepshearing, making and fitting horseshoes, and wrought and ornamental ironwork. Falconry, gun dog and fly-casting demonstrations are staged, as are activity rides by the intrepid Pony Club Display Team, who do mounted acrobatics as though to the manner born. In the horse ring are various show-jumping contests, including the unusual Open Power and Speed Jumping Competition, which may have as many as fifty entrants. If the communion between man and horse which makes for the successful show-jumping, horseracing or three-day event partnership is an extraordinary one, that between man and sheepdog is even more mystical, for there is no physical contact between them. This is nowhere better illustrated than in the sheepdog trials which are a main attraction of the Royal Welsh Show. Standing immobile at one end of the arena, the handler must direct his dog to fetch the sheep from the far end and then drive them through a 'gate' seven yards wide, out over a triangular obstacle course and back into the narrowest of pens.

Summer

MEDIEVAL JOUSTING TOURNEY

The tournament was devised as a sport for underemployed knights by a Geoffroy de Preuilly, who died in 1066. The throng of knights were divided into two teams, who charged at each other with lances levelled. Those who were unseated continued to fight on foot. Though the idea was simply to capture a member of the opposite team, pursuing him into the open countryside if necessary, instances of overenthusiasm and professional fouls were frequent and squires were on hand to carry away the unconscious and the dead. A knight who gave up had to surrender his horse and armour to his captor or pay an appropriate ransom. Some knights made a good living out of

Facing page: the ancient sport of tilting. The knight charges, lance at the ready, at a shield suspended from the cross-piece of a pole. If he hits it cleanly, it will revolve. Extras are on hand to bear the standards (top right) onto the field of tourney and the casualties (top left) away from it. The Black Knight, Sir Guy of Gisbourne (left), rides onto the field in full panoply. His helm represents the phoenix rising from the ashes. In one contest he unseats Richard Earl of Cornwall (above), who then finds himself at the mercy of his opponent (far left).

tournaments. William Marshal, who died in 1219, was the penniless younger son of a minor baron and was attached to the household of the Constable of Tancarville. When his horse died, he borrowed the most unmanageable horse in the Constable's stable and, by repeatedly capturing wealthy opponents in tournaments, made himself rich.

Eventually, objections by the Church brought about

changes to tournament rules. Armour became heavier, lances were blunted and single combat became a feature of the sport. The lance was fitted into a rest on the right breastplate and the two mounted knights met at a slow canter. The aim was to hit your opponent cleanly on the helmet or breastplate and unseat him, whilst avoiding his lance or parrying it with your shield. The horse was controlled using knees and heels alone. These changes made the tournament into a suitable spectator sport for women, who came to encourage and applaud their favourites. Ultimately, tournaments became a cross between a festival and a trade fair and so were also attended by horse dealers, armourers, money lenders and prostitutes. The first recorded international match resulted from a challenge issued by the fourteenth-century Sire de Boucicaut and two companions to the knights of England. The joust lasted for four days, during which each of the three Frenchmen took on twelve successive opponents in turn, without one of the Frenchmen ever being unseated.

Restaging medieval-style jousts in a modern setting

was the inspiration of a man with a background in a circus of long standing. In 1798 a cavalry sergeant major called Philip Astley established Astley's Royal Amphitheatre, with the encouragement of the Prince of Wales and the Duke of York. He put on exhibitions of skilled and trick riding, which he also took all round the country. The tradition was continued by Astley's son and thus Astley's Circus was born. Geoff Winship, whose family had worked for or run Astley's for five generations, began as a trick rider and high-wire acrobat and then studied theatre production. Some twenty years ago, he was invited to produce and direct a medieval jousting tournament for a new entertainment

complex, which he did with a budget that allowed for only four mounted knights. The spectacle originally ran for nineteen weeks and has been growing and developing ever since. Whereas in medieval times knights travelled huge distances to compete in a tournament, the opposite now applies and Winship's tournament does the travelling, with a full cast of medieval characters: jesters, courtiers, ladies and men-at-arms, as well as the statutory knights and squires. The aim is to entertain, but to do so as realistically and authentically as possible. This sometimes involves danger, in addition to strength, skill and supreme riding ability.

Colourful action abounds at the tourney and, whilst the execution (facing page bottom left) is just for show, the blood drawn (facing page top left) in an enthusiastic bout is for real. This mixture of fantasy and reality increases the excitement of the occasion.

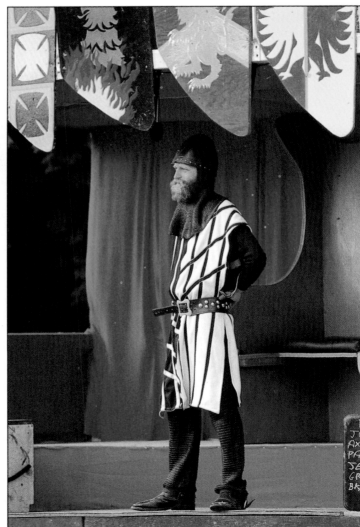

Summer

A DAY BESIDE THE SEA

The Victorians may be credited with inventing the seaside as a place for the mass of people to go on holiday. Before this time, the seaside resort had been the haunt solely of royalty or of the wealthy, who sought alternative destinations when the Napoleonic Wars put a stop to holidaying on the Continent. In 1787, the then Prince of Wales was the first to sample Brighton's sea air. Two years later, his father, George III, was prevailed upon to test the water of Weymouth Bay. The fine Georgian architecture of both towns testifies to the trend that these royals started. By the 1860s the urban middle classes had established their right to an annual summer holiday and they took advantage of the expansion of the railway system to transport themselves, their children and sometimes their servants to the seaside. The excursion train was the invention of a Baptist lay preacher, who, in 1841, persuaded the Midland Counties Railway Company to lay on a special service from Leicester to Loughborough, a round trip of twenty-six miles, for a temperance

meeting. Further trips followed, the enterprising Baptist being paid a percentage on all tickets sold. Twenty years later he expanded his operations to the Continent. The travel agency that he started still bears his name – Thomas Cook and Son. By the 1890s, Yarmouth, Skegness and Blackpool had joined Scarborough and the south coast resorts as holiday destinations and couples sprawled on the sands in full Victorian rig – there was no risk of sunburn in those days. Little, and not so little, girls demurely hoisted their voluminous skirts knee-high to paddle in the sea. The seaside holiday was adopted less enthusiastically in Scotland for a reason that has been admirably summed up by

Molly Weir, writing of her first experience of it: '"Ma Goad," said my mother, when I came out, "look at her. She's blue wi' cauld. Ye stayed in faur too long." "It was great," I said, my teeth chattering. "It was as warm as anything."'

The mystique of the seaside overrides the weather – sunny and warm is admirable, but sunny and cool is endured – and the minor inconveniences – sand gets in your shoes and pebbles hurt the soles of your feet. Lazing around for hours on end is socially acceptable on the beach, but sheer indulgence anywhere else. Thus the English will continue to visit the seaside and to return refreshed by the change of air and routine.

Top left: high noon is braved by two trippers, but the beach is almost deserted by 8 pm (top right). The varied aspects of relaxation by the sea at Selsey, Sussex highlight different British attitudes towards undressing in the sun.

Summer

TRAINING FOR THE BEAT

In 1901, when the first telephone was installed in New Scotland Yard, Headquarters of the Metropolitan Police Force, who patrol over 787 square miles of London and its environs, an old sergeant commented: 'I don't know what we're coming to – if this sort of thing goes on, we'll have the public ringing us up direct!' He was proved right, of course, and today more than 80,000 people make emergency calls to the Yard's Information Room every year. Even more modern technology has computerised the police and heralded many new devices to help in the detection

Top left: cadets on parade and (top right) on the beat. Keeping fit (above centre) and learning self-defence (left) are imperative for today's police officer. Theory is important too (far left). The lanyard (above) indicates a cadet in training.

and prevention of crime. At the same time it calls for increasing specialist knowledge on the part of even the youngest recruits to the force and has inspired crimes that were unheard of a generation ago. Every police officer, as soon as he or she begins normal duty, must be something of a lawyer, teacher, sociologist, technician, security expert, diplomat and traffic engineer. They should also be compassionate, discreet, decisive and courageous. Metropolitan police officers begin their careers with a twenty-week course at Peel

Centre Training School, Hendon. This establishment is named after Sir Robert Peel, who, as Home Secretary, received authority from Parliament in 1829 to form an organised police force. 4 Whitehall Place, conveniently near the Home Office, was chosen as its headquarters. This large house backed onto an ancient court that was once the part of the Royal Palace of Whitehall where the Scottish royal family were housed when visiting the English Court. Indeed, it had been called Scotland Yard since the beginning of the sixteenth century. People entering 4 Whitehall Place by its back door came to refer to the building as Scotland Yard. This name was transferred to the force's second home on the Embankment, completed in 1890. The original name now graces the modern tower block in Broadway, SW1, which is the latest headquarters of the Metropolitan Police Force. New Scotland Yard houses

In the canteen (below far left), cadets can relax, but facing the world (left) requires a more official face. Classroom work (below centre left) is only a part of the training. Cadets also learn through demonstrations (below) and practical work. Incidents are staged (below centre and bottom) and trainees have to cope whilst their colleagues and an instructor stand by to assess their performance.

the specialists of the Criminal Investigation Department, about 1,500 officers divided between a number of branches and squads, including the National Central Office for the Suppression of Counterfeit Currency, the Central Drugs Squad, the Central Cheque Squad, the Central Robbery Squad, the Fraud Squad, the Special Branch and the Anti-Terrorist Branch. At grass roots level there are 2,000 male and female plain-clothes detectives, who work from CID offices in the area's seventy-five divisions.

Early in World War I, women's voluntary organisations formed patrols from amongst their members to safeguard the interests of women and girls in London. In 1919 some of these were absorbed into the Metropolitan force as temporary police officers and in 1922, despite stringent economy measures, public protest ensured that a small number of them were retained and given the full powers of a police constable. Today, all officers may compete equally for promotion to any post and all recruits follow exactly the same initial training course at the Peel Centre.

Summer
COWES WEEK

The Welsh have never been a great seagoing people, perhaps because the Welsh coastline is relatively small compared with the country's landmass. Historically, the Irish have been more concerned with meeting the challenge of the vast Atlantic on one side and with the problems of invaders and emigrants on the other. Whilst there are sailing clubs based on the estuaries in southern Scotland, the sea has from time immemorial been an object of awe as well as a source of economic support to the Scots. Much of the British fishing industry is still centred on Scottish ports. In 1800, when the population of England was five times that of Scotland, there were as many Scottish as English officers in the Royal Navy. The character of the Scottish ship's engineer has passed into British literary folklore. Nevertheless, it can be argued that it has largely been left to the English to uphold that tradition expressed by Ratty to Mole in Kenneth Grahame's children's classic, *The Wind in the Willows*: 'There is nothing – absolutely nothing – half so much worth doing as simply messing about in boats.'

Yacht is a Dutch word in origin, and the term jachtship for a fast vessel or sportsman's boat was first used in the seventeenth century. The first Englishman to catch the sailing bug is said to have been Charles II, who was greatly impressed by the yacht in which he sailed from Breda to Delft in 1660, on the first leg of his journey back to Britain for his restoration as monarch. In consequence, the Dutch decided to present him with a yacht of his own. She was called Mary and was fifty-two feet long. Samuel Pepys inspected it and called it 'one of the finest things that I ever saw for neatness and room in so small a vessel'. The King,

anxious to establish a British yacht-building industry as well as a British craze for yachting, commissioned two others, Jenny for himself and Anne for his brother, the Duke of York, from the shipwright and naval commissioner, Peter Pett. On 1 October 1661, the two yachts were raced against each other on the Thames, the Duke winning the downstream leg from Greenwich to Gravesend and the King winning the return run. The first race away from the Thames appears to have been at a regatta in 1776 at Cowes, a resort on the north coast of the Isle of Wight. In 1778, there was a race from Cowes 'westward round

The Velsheda *(top left) was built in 1932 for the America's Cup. The final day of Cowes Week usually features a match race for Thames Barges (above left). From their moorings in the marina (above centre left) boats sail out across the starting line (above) and into the Solent (top right and above centre).*

the Island for vessels carvel-built not exceeding thirty-five tons register'. As in the early stages of any new sport, it was not long before loopholes were found in the rules. In 1795, for instance, the skipper of one boat 'dismantled' that of his opponent by cutting away the rigging with his cutlass. On 1 June 1815, forty-two members of the leisured and aristocratic classes met at a tavern in London and established the Yacht Club to organise regular races from Cowes between private owners, usually as the result of wagers. The meeting that is known as Cowes Week really began in 1826, when the club instituted races for prizes and cups at its annual regatta. By this time it was known as the Royal Yacht Club, George IV having become a member in 1820, the year of his accession. In the following year, he joined the club vessels in a cruise to the Needles, the westernmost point of the island. His yacht was called

The red ensign (left) is flown by British merchant ships and others not belonging to the Royal Navy. Below left: playing the sport of Sir Francis Drake, against a background of sails. Below: sea cadets.

Split-second timing, as well as tactical skill, are required to avoid collisions whilst taking the fastest course. Above: one holiday-maker at Cowes tests the water in a more gentle fashion.

the Royal George and it was in her that he sailed to Scotland in 1822.

In 1833, with the consent of King William IV, the club was renamed the Royal Yacht Squadron, which it remains to this day. It is the only yacht club in the world allowed to fly the white ensign, because of its connections with the Royal Navy. The last royal voyage under sail was undertaken by Queen Victoria and Prince Albert in 1842, when they sailed to Scotland in the Royal George. This was the famous occasion on which the royal party arrived in Edinburgh from the port of Leith earlier than expected and no one was there to welcome them at the gates of the city

The bubbly atmosphere and spirit of Cowes Week are enjoyed as much by the young (left and below left) as by their elders (below).

The signal flag message in the café window (left) reads 'pier view'. Above: dressed for the elements. Facing page: a battered cap tops the features of a genuine salt.

and present them with the silver keys. So they passed on through the city and out the other side to Dalkeith. Royal patronage of Cowes Week was confirmed when Osborne House, largely designed by Prince Albert in Italianate style and reflecting Queen Victoria's mind and personality, was ready for her to occupy in 1848. It became her favourite house and it was there that she died in 1901. By this time Cowes Week had become an international as well as a royal occasion. According

to a contemporary report: 'The Cowes Week has always been an assemblage of aristocrats, but the year 1894 has eclipsed all previous gatherings. Never have so many yachts graced the beautiful waters of the Solent. A cloud of craft was anchored in Osborne Bay, up the Medina, and right away to Gurnards Bay, and flew every national ensign, American, French and German predominating.' Until 1914 most of the races were for the big cutters and for boats with small ratings,

but after 1918 metre boats came into greater prominence, together with one-designs, races in which all the competitors sail the same make of boat.

The attraction of the Solent, that stretch of water which divides the Isle of Wight from the mainland, as a centre for yacht racing lies not only in the comparative protection that the land to the north and south offers, but also in the fact that the sea is constantly changing direction and pace with the tide. This provides a series of challenges not only at different times of the day but in different parts of the channel. So yachtsmen, especially those in light craft, have the tide as well as the wind to contend with or to take advantage of.

Cowes Week is still a royal occasion and its opening feature is usually the arrival of HMY Britannia. Seven clubs, in addition to the Royal Yacht Squadron, combine to organise the event. They are the Royal Thames Yacht Club, Royal Southern Yacht Club, Royal London Yacht Club, Royal Corinthian Yacht Club, Royal Southampton Yacht Club, Royal Ocean Racing Club, and Island Sailing Club. The 'royal' yacht clubs are entitled to fly a blue, rather than a red, ensign, a privilege that is highly prized and jealously guarded. The event actually lasts ten days and is enlivened on land with concerts given by marching and static bands and ladies' choirs and with various other junketings, culminating in a fireworks' display. Individual clubs also host balls for their members on most nights.

Some twenty-five different classes of yacht will be

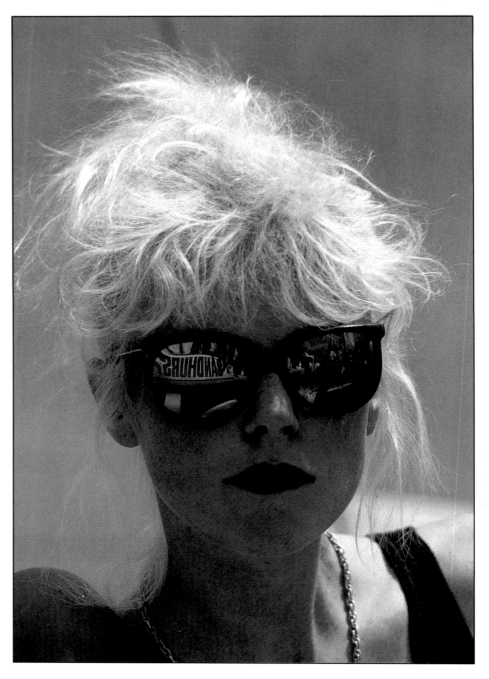

involved in the racing itself, ranging in overall length from a mere sixteen feet to over a hundred feet. Each yacht is classified according to the International Offshore Rule (IOR) or the Channel Handicap System (CHS). IOR is a comprehensive system of measurement whereby the speed of the yacht is assessed and the elapsed time is multiplied to obtain the corrected, or handicapped, time taken for the race. CHS is simpler and is intended for cruising yachts and beginners. In each class there are usually eight races, each over a different course, with the ultimate winner being the

Some spectators adopt various forms of defence against the sun (above, top and far left), whilst others lap it up (top left). Left: sailing with the spinnaker set to take the greatest advantage of the wind.

With the sun sparkling on the water, even landlubbers long to be afloat. The Sigma 33 OOD Class (left) is a one-design race. Below: on board the Velsheda.

boat with the highest set of results overall, calculated on its seven best races. The length of the course may be anything between ten and thirty miles. The basic principles of sailing are concerned with moving the boat relative to the wind by adjusting the sails and handling the rudder. The boat's direction is known as the point of sailing, of which there are, broadly, three. Sailing with the wind behind is called 'running', with the wind from the side 'reaching' and with the wind from in front 'beating'. Beating is achieved by tacking, or sailing on a zig-zag course, towards the objective,

directing the boat so that the wind always fills the sails from the side. According to the circumstances, the sails may be tighter, looser or 'trimmed' to meet the breeze at exactly the required angle. Different techniques are called for when using the helm, whilst offshore the factor of leeway must be taken into account, whereby the tide or current will affect the course which has been set. 'Messing about in boats' is all very well for a time, but sailors soon progress to racing, with its added dimension of vying with other yachts as well as with the elements. Each race is started with a signal, on which the boats cross an imaginary starting line between two sighting points. Each boat will have been manoeuvring to be as close as possible to the line at the off, to be sailing as fast as possible at that moment and to be clear of other boats so that their sails do not blanket another's wind. Each race will involve turning round one or more buoys, so various sailing, as well as tactical, skills will be required, together with a knowledge both of the rules and of the course itself.

Above: the naval signalman at the starting point of the races, with a flotilla of small craft in the background. Left: the crew of Thriller concentrates on bringing the boat back on course as it heels over in the wind.

~ Britain and Her People ~

· CHAPTER 3 ·

AUTUMN

The poet Keats called autumn the 'season of mists and
mellow fruitfulness'. The mists are evident in the Scottish
Highlands (right) and in Horseguards Parade, London (below).
The senior Pearly Queen of London (above) epitomises
mellowness as she attends that celebration of fruitfulness, the
harvest festival, in St Martin-in-the-Fields.

Autumn

THE SHOOT

The appeal of grouse shooting and the contradictory emotions it inspires were once summed up by barrister and artist, V.R. Balfour-Browne. 'It is', he wrote in 1925, 'that desire to kill, strange and primitive perhaps, that gives zest to the whole pursuit. ... To describe the effects of light and shade, of sunshine and shadow, mist and storm, amid the high hills is beyond the power of most pens. ... But alas! So little of the love with which one sees, seems to be infused into the humble record upon paper!' The grouse in question is *Lagopus scoticus*, the red grouse, found especially on the moors of the Scottish Highlands, where heather, its staple diet, flourishes. The grouse appears to be a born

loser. If it is not killed and eaten by animal predators, having been attacked on the ground by foxes or dive-bombed from the air by birds of prey, it is shot and eaten by human predators. Snow and frost wreak havoc in the grouse's nesting season; overgrazing and forestation destroy its breeding grounds; sheep and deer compete with it for food. The birds themselves have a kamikaze habit of flying into fences and killing themselves. Even a good breeding year or a season of inaccurate shooting provides little consolation for the grouse, since the greater their numbers, the more likely is an outbreak of strongylitis. The parasitic strongyle worm attacks the intestines and quickly

Top left: the guns and ammunition. Top right: the red grouse in its habitat. Sandwiches, shortbread and pies (left) may be the staples of the shooting lunch, but the object of the shoot is the bagging of other delicacies (above centre), destined for more formal meals. Above: planning the shoot. Facing page: collecting the prize for a straight shot.

passes from bird to bird via their droppings.

The shooting season opens on 12 August, a day known as the 'Glorious Twelfth'. This term was apparently invented in 1910 by a perceptive parliamentary journalist to describe the mass migration of Members of Parliament northwards during the summer recess to shoot grouse. This sport, a rather uneven contest, has been a national institution in Scotland since Victorian times, when the development of the railway network opened up the Highlands for leisure pursuits and railway companies built lodges on estates in return for a right of way over the land. The 'Glorious Twelfth' itself is celebrated in a curious rite whereby the first grouse casualties of the day are rushed by Landrover, aeroplane and taxi to smart

hotels and restaurants in England. These then vie with each other to be the first to serve the grouse roasted in the traditional manner and accompanied with buttered breadcrumbs and port wine sauce. This, of course, makes complete nonsense of the tradition that a grouse should be hung upside down for several days, to enhance its flavour, before being eaten.

Grouse shooting is an activity for the very rich. A pair of specially designed shotguns will set you back between £35,000 and £40,000. Unless you are fortunate enough to receive a private invitation, you will have to pay highly for the opportunity of taking pot shots at low-flying birds, especially during the first two months of the season. Grouse shooting lasts until 10 December. Charges are usually calculated partly on results and partly by means of a fixed levy based on 'expectations', which is payable whatever the weather and the circumstances. Killing a brace of grouse will cost you a basic sixty to seventy-five pounds depending on the prestige and fecundity of the moor. This price is for driven birds, those disturbed by lines of beaters and persuaded to fly in your direction. The total cost

The bleak Highland moorlands (far left and below) are home to the red grouse and thus to the shoot. Left: a close-up of the landowner, as he sits proprietorially on his moors (below left), where some fifty brace of grouse a day are shot during the season. Bottom: a dog retrieves the kill for his master.

Left: in the butts. Each man has either two guns or one gun with a double barrel. The cartridges, filled with lead pellets, cost a mere £120 per thousand, which is nothing compared with the price of a gun. The stakes mark the arc of fire. There is little shelter on the moors and a hat is essential for preserving body heat. The tweed deerstalker (below left) is a popular choice.

The country may be tough for walking (above), but the scenery is always spectacular (left).

of a week's shooting may be about £3,500, plus VAT and bed and board in a hotel. Charges of £5,000 a day for foreign visitors have been recorded. The process is cheaper if you simply walk over the moor looking for your own prey, guided by a gamekeeper and accompanied by a retriever dog. This calls for greater agility and physical energy, but lacks the traditional hospitality and sociability of the driven shoot.

Much of the success of any shoot depends on the positioning of the butts. The beaters spread out in the form of a crescent, with flags to indicate the direction

of the wind. When a grouse has been disturbed it tends to fly downwind and this has to be taken into account. Once flushed out, the grouse rises with a vigorous flapping of wings and a characteristic croak of alarm before getting up speed and becoming a target. The challenge is an exhilarating one and the competition between guns adds spice to the undoubted pleasure and excitement afforded by the brief moments of activity in the butts. Even the poor shot stands a chance of hitting something, and for those who do miss altogether there is still the invigorating air, the scenery and the companionship. It is considered thoroughly bad form to use any kind of automatic gun, to wear anything but the most sombre of clothes, to wing one of your fellow marksmen or to shoot a beater. There is a break for lunch, which is usually packed in hampers and driven out to the shoot. Originally a formal meal, served by footmen and eaten at trestle tables, set with tablecloths, napkins and silver, today it is much more casual, consisting of food that can be eaten with the fingers, including portions of the statutory cold game pie. Alcohol is bad for the eye as well as the hand and

the hip flask, favourite present for sporting gentlemen, rarely finds its way onto the moor.

Organisations like the Game Conservancy Trust and the Nature Conservancy Council are hard at work monitoring flocks, experimenting with different methods of combatting both disease and the competition from sheep for food and producing statistics, all of which help to preserve the grouse and to predict their numbers in any season. Even so, there appears, despite the fluctuations in numbers from year to year, to be a steady decline overall in the grouse population in Scotland. The days of the grouse shoot

may therefore be numbered, even if the European Commission does not kill it off in the meantime. The draft of one of the Commission's proposed regulations directs that game shall not be killed 'by any method which will contaminate the game carcass in an unacceptable manner or will cause unnecessary suffering to the animal'. This would seem conclusively to rule out a bird slaughtered by a barrage of lead shot. Indeed, some Scottish hotels are already keeping a low profile when serving grouse on the 'Glorious Twelfth', on the grounds that too open a display may result in an invasion of the moors by animal rights protesters.

Top: the shoot's dramatic backdrop is subject to sudden changes in weather as threatening skies (above) blot out the blue. Facing page: the personalities of the shoot: the follower (top left), the gamekeeper (top right) and the participant (bottom).

Autumn

ALTERNATIVE BATH

According to legend, the healing properties of the waters of Bath were first publicised in 860 B.C. when a Celtic prince, Bladud, was banned from the court because of his leprosy and so became a swineherd. His pigs, who also suffered from a skin disease, wallowed one day in a pool of warm water and came out cured. Bladud followed them in and, in due course, was also cured. He dedicated the place to the Celtic god, Sul. Later, the Romans called the place Aquae Sulis and built an elaborate bathing complex on the site, dedicated to Sulis Minerva, combining the original deity with one of their own goddesses. The main Roman bath was not rediscovered until 1879. It now stands as it did then,

Facing page: shop front in one of Bath's pedestrianised shopping lanes. Top left: flowers on the tables are a feature of pubs in Bath. The expansion of the Georgian city led to later architectural developments of a more plebeian nature (top right). Around tea time the deckchairs in the public gardens (above) are abandoned in favour of afternoon tea in the Pump Room (far left), rebuilt in 1795 and recently restored to the elegance of that era. Visitors may also taste the waters here. Left: a typical Sunday occupation in one garden of a Bath suburb.

lined with lead, open to the sky and fed by springs producing 500,000 gallons of water a day at a constant temperature of 49°C. By the seventeenth century Bath had become a haunt of petty criminals, prostitutes, quacks, and gamblers, but, in 1704, it was transformed into an elegant, fashionable resort after Richard 'Beau' Nash became its self-appointed 'Master of Ceremonies'. The city's elegant Georgian plan and architecture were one result of this and remain its chief glory.

Autumn

THE BRAEMAR GATHERING

Although it was Queen Victoria who invested the Braemar Gathering with royal patronage, it was a much earlier ancestor of hers, Malcolm III, known as Canmore, or 'big-headed', who invented it. Malcolm was a warrior king, who spoke English, Latin and Gaelic, but could not read or write any of them. In

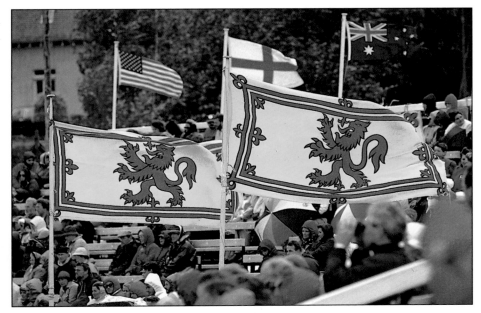

order to select his 'hardiest soldiers and fleetest messengers', he would summon the clans to gather for a competition at the Braes of Mar, as it was then called, an important meeting place from which drove roads spread out in all directions. Soldiers were always needed, as it was Malcolm's habit periodically to invade Northumberland, plundering the countryside and bringing back as slaves those whom he did not kill. Three times he was pursued back to Scotland and forced to submit to the English. When he invaded a

fourth time, he and his son Edward were ambushed and killed by the Earl of Northumberland.

Highland gatherings and the games that so often accompanied them developed as extensions of the fairs and meetings organised by clan chiefs and were by no means confined to the Scottish Highlands. The Antigonish Games in Nova Scotia, Canada, were instituted in 1861 and are still held annually. The first ever recorded annual gathering was held in 1314 in the village of Ceres, Fife, in honour of the local

Facing page: leading the drums and pipes of the 1st Battalion, Gordon Highlanders. Top left: swinging the weight and (above) putting the Braemar Stone. Top right: a piper on parade. Above centre: damp spectators and (above left) the royal family sheltering in their pavilion.

bowmen as they returned victorious from the battle of Bannockburn against the English. This gathering is unique in that it is said to have taken place every year since then, except during the two World Wars. Traditionally, the main event of the day is a horse race, the Ceres Derby, contested by 'big nags, small mokes, spavined mares and an occasional hunter'. After the failure of Bonnie Prince Charlie's rebellion in 1745, the Hanoverian government in Britain introduced a complicated series of measures and laws designed to suppress the clan system. The measures included the Act of Proscription, which forbade the wearing of anything resembling Highland dress on pain of six months in jail, with seven years' transportation for a

On the day after the gathering, the royal party goes to church in Balmoral (below and below far left). Concentration is essential for the sword dance, particularly for the under nines (left). As some athletes await their turn (below left), others relax after the hill race (below centre). Bottom: waiting for the royal party.

second offence. The Act's repeal in 1782 inspired an upsurge of enthusiasm for anything Highland, whether genuine or not, and gatherings and games proliferated. Braemar had already gained some notoriety before the 1745 Rebellion. It was here that in 1715 the Earl of Mar, known as 'Bobbing John', either because of a disability that affected his walking or because of his habit of changing political sides, proclaimed Bonnie Prince Charlie's father King James VIII of England and Scotland, a move which culminated in the battle of Sheriffmuir. In 1817 there was another meeting at Braemar that had the somewhat different purpose of establishing a system of social insurance. The Braemar Wrights Friendly Society, a body of local craftsmen, began holding an annual games to raise funds for widows and orphans and for the maintenance of sick and superannuated members. In 1826 the Society extended its scope to include the preservation of the dress, language and culture of the Highlands, as well as its sporting activities, and became the Braemar Highland Society. The original meetings were known

Facing page top left: wearing of the tartan is favoured by spectators and compulsory for most competitors. Exceptions include the hill runners (facing page bottom right), who have to scramble 2,800 feet up Morrance and back. Their litheness contrasts with the stockier figure required for putting the stone (facing page top right) and heaving the weight over a bar (facing page bottom left).

as the 'Wrights' Walk' and they began with a procession, headed by a pipe band, which wound its way to some suitable spot where members could take part in sporting contests and in piping and dancing competitions.

Queen Victoria attended the Braemar Gathering at Invercauld House in 1848 during her first stay in the Highlands, at the old Balmoral Castle. For the following two years the gathering took place at Braemar Castle. She wrote in her diary for 12 September 1850: 'There were the usual games of putting the stone, throwing the hammer and caber, and racing up the hill of Craig

Cheunnich, which was accomplished in less than six minutes and a half; and we were all much pleased to see our gillie Duncan, who is an active, good-looking young man, win. He was far before the others the whole way. It is a fearful exertion. Mr Farquharson brought him up to see me afterwards. Eighteen or nineteen started, and it looked very pretty to see them run off in their different coloured kilts, with their white shirts (the jackets or doublets they take off for all the

games), and scramble up through the wood, emerging gradually at the edge of it, and climbing the hill.' What she did not record, if indeed she knew, is that several of the contestants were spitting blood after the race and the winner, who became a gamekeeper, never properly recovered from that exhausting race. As a result it was discontinued, to be reinstated later in its present gentler form, the record for the course being twenty-four minutes twenty-eight seconds. In 1866

Top left: a competitor.
Above left: putting the weight. Judges check the validity of the throw and then measure the distance (above).

Queen Victoria conferred royal patronage on the society, and it became the Braemar Royal Highland Society. She contributed regularly to its funds and kept up a firm interest in the Braemar Gathering itself. The present site was a gift from the Duke of Fife in 1906.

The former castle at Balmoral was knocked down in 1852, immediately after the estate had been bought by Prince Albert as a present for his wife. The new Balmoral Castle was ready for occupation three years later and it has remained the Scottish holiday residence of the Royal Family ever since, their visits usually coinciding with the Braemar Gathering. Indeed, it is the regular attendance of the royal party that has given the gathering its international prestige. Among the 20,000 spectators who assemble on the appointed Saturday in September are many from outside Scotland, particularly from those traditional Scottish outposts, England, Australia, Canada, New Zealand and the USA. It is a great occasion and it matters little that the conglomeration of gentry and royalty, the well-cut tweeds and the tartan kilts bear as little relationship to

Below: a Highland bonnet decorated with a clan badge bearing the motto Dum spiro spero, *'While I breathe, I hope.'*

The intricate pattern of the sword dance (above left) is further enlivened by the colourful dress of the young competitors. The concentration of the Gordon Highlanders (above) matches that of the hammer thrower (left). Throwing the hammer Braemar style means using a hammer with a solid shaft, like those used in the mid-nineteenth century. The modern version has a ball on the end of a wire with a double handle.

of variegated colour since all competitors, except those in running and jumping competitions, must wear Highland dress. In addition to the hill race, there are more traditional track events at various distances, handicap and scratch, open and for local competitors only. There is a 'running high leap' and a 'running long leap', as well as the hop, step and jump. One special feature of those traditional Highland field events,

Left: C.F. McIntosh, President of the Braemar Royal Highland Society. Judging the pipers (below) is a serious business, whatever their age.

normal life in Scotland as the well-heeled crush, the morning suits and dashing hats of Royal Ascot bear to ordinary life in England.

Braemar itself is a scattered village situated 1,100 feet above sea level, at the confluence of the Clunie Water and the Dee. On the occasion of the gathering in September there is a lush green surface to the arena of the Princess Royal and Duke of Fife Memorial Park, named after Princess Louise, eldest daughter of the Prince of Wales and later Princess Royal, and her husband, who was created Duke of Fife on their marriage in 1889. The hills surrounding Braemar are alive with purple heather. Traditionally, the programme begins at 9.30 am with the open competition for the *Piobaireach*, or bagpipe playing, which goes on throughout the day and does not finish until some time after the last event in the arena. Pipers of all ages play their way through marches, strathspeys, and reels. Dancers, some of them under nine years old, compete at the highland fling, the reel, the solo dance, the sword dance, the sailor's hornpipe and 'Will You Go to the Barracks, Johnnie?' Almost every event is a riot

putting the shot, throwing the hammer and tossing the caber, is that these are performed with implements made to the specifications of the Braemar Royal Highland Society. The 'shot' is a stone, the hammer has a solid shaft and the caber with which the ultimate open event, the Braemar Caber, is contested is nineteen feet nineteen inches long, and weighs 132 pounds. There is also a Braemar speciality event, heaving a fifty-six-pound weight over a bar with one hand. The Braemar Gathering constitutes the most colourful, the most active and the noisiest expression of acclamation of Her Majesty the Queen as the Sovereign of Scotland and the chieftain of the gathering itself. It is significant of the parochial pride of the Scots that, in official announcements and records of the event, the Prince of Wales is referred to as the Duke of Rothesay and the Princess as the Duchess of Rothesay. The formal salute to the sovereign and her family is given in a glittering march past of some dozen massed pipe bands, representing police forces, districts and social clubs from all over Scotland and augmented by the drums and pipes of a military regiment.

Above left: weighing-in for the tug-o'-war and (above) preparing to pull in the Inter-Services Unit Championship. Which way will it fall? Everybody watches after the caber's been tossed (facing page top left), while the piper plays (facing page top right). Facing page bottom: the under 16 handicap sack race, keenly contested.

Autumn

EXCAVATING THE WALL

Hadrian's Wall, which once ran unbroken for seventy-three miles right across the country from Bowness on the Solway Firth to Tynemouth, is the grandest Roman monument in Britain and one of the most impressive antiquities of the entire Roman Empire. The extension and retention of an empire that once incorporated what is now England, Spain, France, half of Germany, the territory on either side of the river Danube, Italy, Greece, the Middle East and a wide strip along the coast of North Africa necessarily involved the establishment of boundaries and the construction of defensive walls. The purpose of Hadrian's Wall, conceived by the globe-trotting Emperor Hadrian and built between 122 and 127 A.D. under the supervision of the governor of Britain, Aulus Platorius Nepos, was to keep a whole invasion force at bay. The Caledonians, the native tribes to the north, were finally defeated by Agricola at Mons Graupius in 84 A.D., but they had never succumbed to Roman rule and had been left to regroup unmolested. After all, to those brought up in the Mediterranean climate, the Scottish winters must

have seemed as endless as the glens were impenetrable under snow. The Wall was intended to keep the Caledonians where they were. It was an elaborate defensive system, comprising a V-shaped ditch up to five metres deep and twelve metres wide, dug where necessary out of solid rock. Behind this was built a battlemented wall five metres high and about three metres wide. There were seventeen forts along its length. In addition, towers were erected every mile and between each pair of towers there were two fortified turrets. The forts do not appear to have been part of the original plan and were added as the wall itself was being built. Each fort was capable of housing 1,000

men. Between the forts and the military road that skirted the wall on its southern side, civilian settlements grew up, squalid tangles of dwellings, taverns, and shops, in which lived the soldiers' families, army veterans and hangers-on. Hadrian's successor, Antoninus, extended the boundary of the province of Britain northwards, and a turf wall was built to mark the new boundary. Twice, the northern tribes broke through it and wreaked havoc in the lands beyond. Hadrian's Wall, however, though often damaged, stood firm, until it was finally abandoned in about 400. That so much of it still remains is a reflection of the skill and spirit of the men who constructed and defended it.

Hadrian's Wall at Housesteads Fort (these pages), Northumberland, was built on the hilliest section of the wall. The civilian settlement that grew up outside the fort is still being excavated.

Autumn

AN ENGLISH PREPARATORY SCHOOL

Some twenty years ago there was a national crisis in education when comprehensive schooling, with its non-selective entry requirements, was imposed as the secondary stage of state education in England and Wales. On the one hand, the establishment of larger schools into which all state pupils automatically passed at the end of their primary years did away with the dreaded eleven-plus examination and the invidious stigmatisation of pupils whose results once assigned them to secondary modern or technical schools, rather than to the more academically-inclined grammar schools. On the other hand, it was feared that

comprehensive schooling might result in the erosion of academic standards. Today over ninety per cent of the state's secondary school population is educated in comprehensive schools, which take pupils without reference to their aptitudes or abilities. The schools may be organised locally on a one-, two- or three-tier basis, but the principles remain the same. The arguments of the 1970s have been largely submerged, if not actually forgotten, in new controversies about the National Curriculum, teachers' duties and pay and educational standards. Alongside this state system, some might say aloof from it, is the private education system, which caters for some seven per cent of the school-age population in an atmosphere of increasing controversy and uncertainty. The mere idea that a different system of schooling is available to the privileged few simply because they can pay for it is anathema to many. Others argue that parental choice is a justifiable option which should be recognised as well as exercised and that parents who send their children to independent

schools still support the state education system as taxpayers. Although there are bursaries to help parents who cannot afford the fees and government- and local authority-assisted places for children whose needs cannot adequately be met within the state system, selection to independent secondary schools is inevitably weighted in favour of those children who are already in the system. The 200 or so, traditionally all-male, establishments known as the public schools take pupils, usually at thirteen, through a standardised Common Entrance examination. Feeding the public schools, and their equivalents for girls, are the mainly single-sex preparatory, or prep, schools. Happily, though, the macho image of the public school is being eroded. All but a few diehards now admit girls to the sixth form and more and more are becoming fully co-educational, which would have been unthinkable in the 1970s. Co-education alone, however, does not necessarily spell equal opportunity. Perhaps the advocates of comprehensive education got it right?

Some independent schools are denominational and some run their own preparatory schools, which test pupils before entry. Ampleforth College, a Roman Catholic public school in Yorkshire, is an example of both. Its prep school, Gilling Castle (these pages), is run by monks, with a full-time lay staff and a lay headmaster. The surroundings are historic and the boys eat in the Elizabethan Great Chamber. This was lost in 1929 to the predatory collecting habits of Randolph Hearst, but was recovered and re-installed after his death in 1951.

Autumn

A Pearlies' Thanksgiving

As recorded in Deuteronomy 16, Moses said: 'Thou shalt observe the feast of tabernacles seven days, after that thou hast gathered in thy corn and thy wine: And thou shalt rejoice in the feast, thou, and thy son, and thy daughter, and thy manservant, and thy maidservant, and the Levite, the stranger, and the fatherless, and the widow, that are within thy gates.' The feast of tabernacles reappeared in British folklore as the harvest home supper, variously called in different parts of the country the horkey, mell-supper, kirn feast and clyack, and was celebrated alongside Jewish and Christian observances associated with the gathering in of the harvest. However, right up to recent times, there also survived echoes of

A church has stood on the site of St Martin-in-the-Fields, Trafalgar Square, since at least the thirteenth century. The present church (left) was built in 1722-26 by James Gibbs. Grace Elwood-Smith (above), seen here with her daughter, is a descendant of one of the earliest members of the association. The title of pearly king is passed down from father to eldest son. There are today about forty full members, the youngest being eighteen, the earliest age at which it is legal to collect money for charity. Including princes and princesses, the total number is about 350. The pearlies decorative techniques are legendary and their outfits look good from front or back (far left).

mysterious, and sometimes dark, rites which go back even further. Many of these are to do with the cutting of the last sheaf of the standing corn, to which, until the invention of the combine harvester, special significance was attached, especially in northern and western regions of Britain.

The last sheaf was known by many titles, including the Neck, the Gander's Neck or the Mare, in England;

the Maiden in Scotland; and *Caseg Fedi,* or harvest mare, and *Guerach,* or hag, in Wales. The privilege of cutting it was often awarded to the most attractive unmarried girl on the farm, or there might be a contest of skill, each reaper in turn flinging his sickle at it until it fell. In some parts of England, the man who got the Neck then ran off at top speed to the farmhouse, where a milkmaid, forewarned by the cheers, stood with a pail of water at the ready. If the reaper managed to get into the house without being drenched, he was allowed to kiss the milkmaid. The final sheaf might then be made into a corn dolly, being cut and woven

Pearlies' get-togethers are jolly occasions (above left). Members collect for charity in their own free time and can be seen at most public events in the London area. The glorious baskets of fruit and vegetables (above) brought for the thanksgiving service are indicative of their generosity. Left: each member has the name of their borough embroidered on their back.

prettiest village girl, dressed in white with a yellow sash and wearing a straw hat decked with corn and flowers, was often set on the leading horse, another hangover from the pagan celebration of the harvest. The uproarious Scottish singing game, Babbity Bowster, which marked the end of the harvest merrymaking, has distinctly sexual overtones. Scotland's national poet, Robert Burns, wrote several songs about the more private goings-on at harvest time, notably the touching *Comin thro' the Rye*, with its concluding verse: 'Gin a body meet a body / Comin thro' the grain; / Gin a body kiss a body, / The thing's a body's ain'. In the Scottish Highlands, old pagan religious beliefs survived into Christian times and were even adapted to a Christian pattern. Thus, Gaelic incantations survived in which there was a mingling of pagan and Christian elements. Such a one was the Reaping Blessing, still being recited at the end of the nineteenth century, which invoked 'Michael head of hosts ... Mary fair-skinned branch of grace ... Bride smooth-white of ringleted locks ... Columba of the graves and tombs'.

The same intermingling of rites occurred in English churches, too, the corn dolly being welcomed with a peal of church bells and solemnly blessed. Sometimes

Below: pearl earrings and choker complement the 'pearls' of dress and hat. Bottom: children and grandchildren follow the pearly tradition, dressing the part from the earliest age. Below left: members sparkle like their clothes.

to resemble the form of a woman and adorned with ribbons and paper trimmings to represent clothes. The Maiden, as the last sheaf was called in Scotland, was kept by the farmer as the embodiment of the young and fruitful spirit of the harvest. Another figure, made from the stalks of an earlier reaping and called *Cailleach*, or old wife, was passed from farmer to farmer, remaining with the one who was the last to finish his harvesting. The English corn dolly, known as the Ivy Girl or Corn Baby, was brought back to the farm by waggon, attended by all the harvest workers, playing any musical instruments they had to hand and singing. The

it was even fixed above the chancel arch. Such traditions ceased with the Reformation, when the whole idea of a harvest service also lapsed. The service is said to have been revived in 1843 by the Reverend Hawker, Vicar of Morwenstow, when he wrote to his congregation inviting them to receive the Sacrament 'in the bread of the new corn'. Within thirty years, the Harvest Thanksgiving Service had become a feature of the Church's calendar. Today, there are still many country churches, especially in the corn belt, which are festooned with bunches of grapes and flowers at harvest time. Fruit and vegetables adorn the pulpit and the font. Baskets of produce stand along the aisle. The

The community spirit of the pearlies is evident in their thanksgiving service. Although Henry Croft originally involved all the boroughs of London in his perpetual charity campaign, the Pearlies have become particularly associated with the tradition of the Cockney costermongers.

corn dolly may have been superannuated, but its spirit survives in decorative devices of wheat and barley and loaves baked in the form of sheaves. The spectacular church of St Martin-in-the-Fields, in London's Trafalgar Square, is the official base and church of the Pearly Kings and Queens, who hold their annual service of Harvest Thanksgiving in it. The Pearly Kings and Queens were the brainchild of Henry Croft, who died in 1930. He was born in King's Cross, but was soon orphaned, becoming a member of the original Dr Barnardo's Home in Commercial Road. Still uneducated when he left the Home at thirteen, he became a rat-catcher and street-sweeper. He also wanted to help other Barnardo children. Noticing that the sequins that French sailors wore on their lapels attracted attention, he sewed pearl buttons all over his suit to catch the eye of the public as he collected money. The ploy was an immediate success and over the next twenty years he recruited a couple of people from each of the twenty-eight old metropolitan boroughs to help him raise funds for charity.

Autumn

AN INDIAN SUMMER, EAST ANGLIA

East Anglia, that region of flat countryside, wide skies and brilliant seascapes, was once a Saxon kingdom. As early as the third century A.D., Saxon pirates were accustomed to conducting their business in East Anglia on a regular basis. Silent raids were the pirates' speciality. They sailed across the open sea by day and into the following night and then, under cover of the darkness, rowed up a tidal river, descended on a sleeping village, took what they wanted and returned home on the morning's offshore breeze. Later, they simply came and stayed and so it was that, in about 500, the area comprising Norfolk, Suffolk, Cambridgeshire and the Isle of Ely was formed into one of the seven Saxon kingdoms. According to the Venerable Bede, who was writing about 200 years later, its first king was called Wuffa and his dynasty the Wuffings. After several centuries of dispute, East Anglia became, under Canute, one of the four great earldoms of his kingdom, the others being Northumbria, Mercia and Wessex. The old Anglo-Saxon kingdom was overthrown by William the Conqueror near

The lonely expanses of the north Norfolk coast (top left) contrast with the lively waterways of the Norfolk Broads (top right). There are more windmills in East Anglia than in any other part of Britain. They were used for grinding corn or to operate drainage machinery. Blickling Hall (left) was built in Norfolk between 1616 and 1625 for Sir Henry Hobart, a notable chief justice during the reign of James I and Keeper of the Great Seal to Charles I when he was Prince of Wales.

Hastings on 14 October 1066 and the Norman era began. The coast of Suffolk was rather different in Anglo-Saxon, Norman and even more recent times from the way it is now because it is constantly eroded by the sea. Nowhere has this happened more spectacularly than at Dunwich, south of Southwold. At the time of the Norman conquest, Dunwich was a flourishing town of considerable size, with a number of churches and even, once, a cathedral. From about

1070, the sea claimed almost everything, the tower of the last medieval church finally toppling in 1919.

Local chalkstone flints, the clay from which multi-toned bricks were manufactured and the wood from the local forests that formed frames for the houses all influenced the development of East Anglia's distinctive architecture. Whilst the wool trade, until its collapse in the seventeenth century, subsidised some of Suffolk's most glorious monuments, notably the Church of the

Holy Trinity at Blythburgh, the Church of the Holy Trinity at Long Melford and the Church of St Peter and St Paul at Lavenham. Many of Lavenham's houses still have their original timber frames. Tudor and Jacobean houses abound in East Anglia and, if Blickling Hall in Norfolk is the showpiece, there are many more modest dwellings of the same period, often still lived in by the descendants or successors of the original owners.

Inevitably, agriculture replaced the wool trade as East Anglia's main industry, complementing the traditional fishing industry centred on Great Yarmouth and Lowestoft, both of which today double up as popular seaside resorts. Norfolk, however, remains

Left: an old Broads sailing barge refitted as a mobile houseboat. The lakes which constitute the Broads are man-made, formed from pits left by turf cutters in ages past.

Centre left: some of the caravans in a park on the cliffs by Cromer seem perilously close to the edge. The sea hereabouts is notoriously treacherous and the Cromer lifeboat is justly famous for its life-saving. The coastal vegetation and wide-open spaces at Cley-next-the-Sea (above centre) hide the bird-watchers on the pebble beach (above). Left: the picture-postcard village of Cavendish in Suffolk. The church tower is fourteenth century.

comparatively unpopulated. Its vast expanses enclose the Broads, a unique combination of lakes, rivers and canals, frequented by boating and sailing enthusiasts and by professional and amateur naturalists. Along its northern fringe lies a series of small seaside resorts and coastal villages – Hunstanton, Wells, Blakeney, Cley-next-the-Sea, Sheringham and Cromer, a medieval village that developed into a Regency holiday resort and the centre of the county's crab trade. East Anglia

has remained comparatively unspoilt because its geographical position means that it is not on the way to anywhere else in Britain. The region is rich in villages and has inspired many notable paintings and painters, amongst whom are local artists Constable and Gainsborough and also Steer and Turner. It has also prompted many works of descriptive literature from such contemporary authors as Adrian Bell, Ronald Blythe and George Ewart Evans.

Autumn

GOLF AT ST ANDREW'S

Whilst there is some evidence that golf originated in Holland, national pride requires that it was first played on those curious stretches of uneven grassland which run alongside Scotland's sandy beaches and are known locally as links. The sandpits and dunes were regarded as natural hazards and were pressed into service as bunkers and traps. The famous Old Course at St Andrews, on the coast of Fife, is unique in that its double greens mirror another feature of these original courses. In the early days, golfers set out and played as far as they could, about nine holes' distance, and then turned about and played back to the start, using the same greens and holes as on the outward leg. The

Top left: playing to the green. Each hole is clearly marked with all the relevant information (top right). The Old Course at St Andrews is a public course, owned by a trust representing the Royal and Ancient Golf Club and local ratepayers. Any serious golfer is entitled to play on it, although between June and September there is a visitors' ballot. Above and above left: tending the 18th fairway, through which snakes the Swilcan Burn. A public road, Granny Clark's Wynd, crosses the fairway a hundred yards farther on. The portico (above left) belongs to the historic Club House. Left: waiting to drive.

earliest historical reference to the game is in an edict of James II of Scotland, banning the playing of both football and golf in favour of the more useful pursuit of archery. The edict was not successful. Neither were several similar remonstrances made by his successors. James IV gave up the unequal struggle and took up the game himself, and his son, James V, was a notable player. It is said that Mary, Queen of Scots, also swung a useful club, and it was during a round on the links at Leith in 1641 that Charles I heard of the Irish rebellion. The game is thus indubitably both ancient and royal, fully justifying the title given by twenty-two 'noblemen and gentlemen' to the club they founded at St Andrews in 1754. The Royal and Ancient Golf Club is not the oldest golf club, an honour held by the Royal Blackheath, founded in 1608, but it is the governing body of the game. The Old Course itself was gradually developed from the natural links beside the shore. There have been considerable improvements to golfing equipment in modern times, but the Old Course, apart from minor adjustments, has been allowed to retain its original quirks as well as its character and it is a mark of the skill of its original designers that the present record, albeit over the extended championship course, is still only six strokes better than the round achieved in 1897 by Willie Auchterlonie playing with a gutta-percha ball! The Old Course has picturesque names for each hole, including Ginger Beer, Hole o' Cross, Heathery Hole, Cartgate, and for many of its more prominent hazards: beware the Principal's Nose, Deacon Sime, the Grave, the Beardies, the Coffins, Walkinshaw's Bunker, named after a regular player who never failed to find it each time he played the 13th, Kruger, Mrs Kruger on the other side of the fairway and Hell Bunker. The 17th is the notorious Road Hole, to reach which the better

For the less energetically inclined there is the Ladies' Putting Green (left) beside the second tee, where matches are played as seriously as on the course itself.

players first drive over the wide angle of the wall of the Old Course Hotel. Immediately behind the green, and in play, is the road itself. By way of an extra hazard, a vast bunker eats into the green. Many players, having played safely onto the green, have then been mesmerised into putting into the bunker. The 18th has seen many famous finishes, but none more enthralling than the Open Championship of 1970. Doug Sanders, faced with a downhill put of two and a half feet to win, missed it. Everyone came back the next day for the play-off between him and Jack Nicklaus. They reached the 18th, 358 yards and par 4, all square. Sanders drove safely. Nicklaus drove his ball right through the green and into a patch of long grass just below the Club House. From there he chipped to within two yards of the hole and sank the put for the match.

A caddie (above and left) is as important an asset to the occasional visitor as he is to the championship player. His advice, especially on as hazardous a course as St Andrews, where the sea breezes cause all manner of extra problems, can be invaluable to someone unfamiliar with these.

Autumn

CAMBRIDGE, THE BACKS

Britain's two oldest universities, Oxford and Cambridge, both had their earliest colleges, Peterhouse in Cambridge and Balliol, Merton and University Colleges in Oxford, established in the thirteenth century, although Oxford is generally accepted as the older of the two. Peterhouse was endowed by Hugh de Balsham, Bishop of Ely, in 1284. The town of Cambridge grew as the Romans developed a previous Celtic settlement on a low hill beside the River Cam, which they called Granta. In Saxon times it became a market town and in the eleventh century it was a Norman military base. In 1209, the first students migrated to Cambridge from Oxford, where they had settled after being ordered back from the Sorbonne in Paris by Henry II.

verges on just one college, Magdalen, and the Isis on none, the river Cam at Cambridge, to the west of the city centre, backs onto no less than seven colleges. Indeed the lawns and gardens which slope gently down to it are known collectively as the Backs. The buildings of Queens' and St John's Colleges rise from the river bank itself. Any analogy with Venice at this point is reinforced by a look-alike Bridge of Sighs linking the old and new buildings of St John's, whilst the wooden Mathematical Bridge of Queens' College, constructed in 1749 without the use of a single nail, continues to defy belief, if not science.

The Cambridge University system, like that of Oxford, is college based, although there is a central

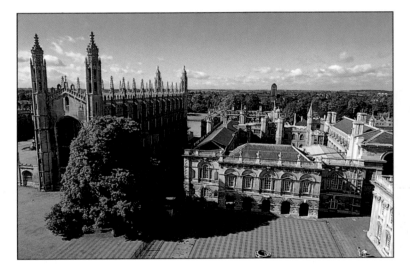

The king feared that English students in France would be tainted by the influence of his opponent, Archbishop Thomas Becket, who had found refuge in France. Several centuries passed before another university was founded in England, an Act of Parliament creating Durham University in 1832. In the meantime, however, no less than four universities had been established in Scotland, with its much smaller area and population. These were St Andrews (1411), Glasgow (1451), Aberdeen (1495) and Edinburgh (1583). Whilst there may be little to choose today between the universities of Oxford and Cambridge, there is a marked difference in the atmosphere of these two historic university towns. Outside the cloistered, academic calm of Oxford an industrial wilderness stretches for miles and merges imperceptibly with satellite suburbs. Cambridge, on the other hand, in spite of its modern technology-based industries, is still at heart a very beautiful market town, set amidst the Cambridgeshire countryside. In addition, whilst of Oxford's two rivers the Cherwell

One of the best ways to see the Backs is from a punt, managed Cambridge style (left), of course. A trip may take you beneath the dipping branches of the willow trees along the bank (top left and above centre), past King's College (top right) or under the Bridge of Sighs, St. John's College (facing page). Above left: King's College Chapel dwarfs the Old Schools. Above: the view upstream from Clare Bridge, surprisingly punt and people free.

administration, including such old-established central university buildings as the Senate House, Old Schools and the university church, St Mary-the-Great, whose chimes were composed in 1793 and were later copied for Big Ben in London. The punt is the traditional leisure craft of the universities of both Oxford and Cambridge. A trip down the gently flowing Cam along the Backs from the Mathematical Bridge at Queens' College will take us next past King's College, founded by Henry VI in 1441, the year after he established Eton College as a school. The chief glory of King's, and the most impressive building at either of the two great universities, is the fifteenth-century chapel. Indeed, with the spectacular, soaring tracery of its fan vaulting and the exquisite stained glass of its interior, the chapel is regarded by some critics as the supreme architectural monument in the Gothic style anywhere in Europe. Beyond King's stands Clare College, founded in 1326 as University Hall. Clare Bridge was built in 1640 and is the oldest in the city. Trinity Hall, which retains its original name to distinguish it from its neighbour, Trinity College, was founded in 1350 by the Bishop of Norwich and was initially a training institute for priests. It has the finest surviving Elizabethan library in the country and keeps some of the books still chained to their shelves. Trinity College was founded in 1336 by Edward III as King's Hall and re-founded under its present name by Henry VIII in 1546. Thomas Nevile,

Above left: window shopping for academic robes. Two footbridges (left) link Trinity Hall and Trinity College with the west bank of the River Cam. Top: music while you punt as a folk dance group takes to the water. Above: even being a passenger is thirsty work.

College, founded in 1542 and for many years the only college on the west bank of the Cam. Pepys left his personal collection of books, 3,000 of them, and the shorthand manuscripts of his diaries, covering the momentous years 1660 to 1669, to the college library. Nobody took any notice of them until a diary by Pepys's friend, John Evelyn, turned up in a laundry basket in the Evelyn family home in 1818 and was promptly published. During the nineteenth century, members of the college were responsible for seeing through the press several edited transcripts of Pepys's diary, but it was not until 1970-77 that the full, unexpurgated version was made public. There are twenty-eight Cambridge colleges in all, the most recent foundation being Robinson College in 1977.

head of Trinity in the reign of Elizabeth I, built the Great Court, the largest courtyard of any university in the world. Just before the river swings to the right and flows under St John's Bridge, built to a design of Sir Christopher Wren's in about 1710, there comes into view another construction of record size. When New Court was built for St John's College, originally founded by Lady Margaret Beaufort in 1511, on the west bank of the river in 1825-31, it was the largest building of any Cambridge college. The Bridge of Sighs, built in 1831, links it to the older college buildings.

Samuel Pepys was an undergraduate of Magdalene

All now take students of both sexes except New Hall and Newnham which admit women only. To the Cambridge resident, university life seems to continue throughout most of the year, the undergraduates and their bicycles being replaced in the long vacation by summer students and their bicycles.

Autumn

BRADFORD, COMMUNITIES AND CULTURE

The vast county that was once known simply as Yorkshire is now divided into three, prosaically called North, South and West Yorkshire. Their total population is about one-tenth that of England and Wales combined. Bradford, in West Yorkshire, was the epitome of Victorian industrial Britain in decline, but is now busy wiping out the past and revitalising itself as a vibrant centre of modern culture. Once, rows of smoke-blackened houses, built back-to-back, surrounded the great wool mills, whilst elsewhere in the city ornate buildings proclaimed the flamboyance and civic pride of their Victorian perpetrators. Bradford was the first town in England to have a school board,

school medical and dental services and school meals, while Saltaire, built by the industrialist Sir Titus Salt in 1853 around his alpaca mill three miles from the city centre, was one of the first model villages in the world. The back-to-back houses largely remain, homes still for Bradford's cosmopolitan population, most recently for the Asian immigrants who now represent over an eighth of the town's population. Much of the extravagant Victorian architecture survives, too, the facades scrubbed and smokefree now and the interiors

either restored to their former glory or redeveloped for new purposes. Salt's mill is being transformed into a leisure centre and already displays a priceless collection of paintings by Bradford-born David Hockney. Bradford's civic pride took a battering in the 1960s and 1970s in particular, and public tragedies and political and cultural controversies have continued to disturb the community and to make national headlines, but there are changes in the air. In the early 1980s unemployment in Bradford stood at twenty per cent.

Top left and above left: the modern generation of Britons. Old industrial homes (top right) still house the new industrial workers. Above centre: cultivating good public relations.

Amidst the general drabness of one residential area (far left), the brightly painted drainpipes (below left) and the primary colours of the children's dress (left and below) provide a welcome splash of colour. Over the last century and more, Bradford has welcomed immigrants from Ireland, Germany, the eastern European countries, Italy, and, more recently, the Caribbean and Asia. Of the present 60,000 Asian immigrants, two thirds are Muslims, which makes Bradford a focus of Islam in Britain. Living conditions may have changed and houses extended upwards, but the general appearance of the terraces remains as it was when they were built to accommodate incoming workers during the Industrial Revolution.

It is now eight per cent. The city's science park is rivalled in Britain only by a similar enterprise in Cambridge. The European Community has donated £200 million to a reconstruction programme. The refurbished Alhambra Theatre is due to be the centre of an eighty-million-pound development. Bradford has housed the National Museum of Photography, Film and Television since 1983 and now welcomes six million tourists a year. Haworth, bleak shrine to the Brontës, is no longer the area's only cultural attraction.

Autumn

HIKING AND HAWKING IN THE DALES

The three counties of Yorkshire constitute between them roughly one eighth of the total area of England. The Yorkshire Dales National Park was so designated in 1954 and is, after the Lake District, England's largest conservation area. It stretches south into Brontë country and includes much of the Pennines, that dark range of hills along which the Pennine Way runs between Derbyshire and Scotland. In contrast to the wild, craggy moors over which Emily Brontë roamed freely as a child and which inspired her grim masterpiece, *Wuthering Heights*, the limestone of the Pennine chain to the north encourages the proliferation of short, bright green grass that nourishes

Facing page: intrepid hikers stride along a road in the Yorkshire Dales National Park. The untamed beauty of the Dales (top right) is occasionally traversed by something more permanent than hikers, such as a railway viaduct (above). Remaining pictures: peregrine falcons, used to hunt rabbits. Though falconry was a royal sport, there was in the sixteenth century a strictly imposed closed season, to protect the interests of farmers. Different kinds of hunting birds were allotted according to the handler's status. The peregrine falcon was originally the proper bird for an earl. Sparrow hawks were for priests, whilst ladies had to make do with a merlin, or pigeon-hawk.

the sheep whose wool was once the main source of the industrial wealth of Bradford and other towns. Between these two extremes lie expanses of heather, wooded valleys, tumbling streams and rocky falls. The spectacular countryside is intersected by narrow, winding roads and ancient drystone walls and dotted with small villages of grey stone cottages with slate roofs. Those for whom leisure is a much more serious and energetic business than merely touring around in a car and gazing at the breathtaking views can enjoy many activities in the Dales. Hiking, whether or not combined with archaeological, ornithological or botanical interests, fishing, pony trekking, rock-climbing and potholing are just a few possibilities. Falconry, one of the more recent Dales pursuits, is one of Britain's most ancient – there are records of its practice in England in the eighth century A.D. The term 'hawking' is used for the practice of falconry in the field.

Autumn

A YORKSHIRE CATTLE MARKET

It is life in the industrial towns and mining areas of Yorkshire that has largely contributed to the image of the Yorkshireman as tough, bluff and craggy. Yorkshiremen are also proud and can be obdurate. Yorkshire County Cricket Club not only refuses to take advantage of the rule that allows the inclusion of an overseas player in every county team, but it also adheres doggedly to the self-imposed regulation that restricts its players to those actually born within the confines of the county. Pregnant wives with cricket-loving husbands are thus unwilling to venture over the border as their time comes near. 'To come Yorkshire'

over someone means to bamboozle them or to defeat them in a battle of wits. When two or more Yorkshiremen are in competition with each other they might cover themselves with the phrase, 'I's Yorkshire too', meaning 'I am as sharp as you and I am not going to be taken in'. The embodiment of the phrase can be observed at any livestock market, especially when the animals are being auctioned. In Yorkshire, agriculture, like everything else, has always been taken very seriously. Indeed, the Dales area of North Yorkshire and the North Peak area of West and South Yorkshire are two of the sixteen farming regions in Britain which the Government has designated 'environmentally sensitive', because of the regions' landscape, historic significance and value as a natural habitat. Outside the industrial and mining centres, the Yorkshire countryside is a generous mixture of the wild and the farmed, the moorland often studded with smallholdings whose original owners cultivated a small part of the moor, but also practised hill grazing to make agricultural ends meet. Elsewhere, large areas were enclosed in the late eighteenth and nineteenth centuries and made into arable farmland. Rising out of the moorland of the North York Moors National Park are the Cleveland Hills, purple with heather in August, golden in October

as the bracken turns. Hereabouts originated the Cleveland Bay, claimed to be the oldest established breed of horse in England. Wensleydale, a gentle, fertile valley that takes its name from what was once its market town but is now a mere village, is noted not only for its cheese, but also for its breed of sheep with their heavy fleeces of long, lustrous wool. It was wool that gave Yorkshire its original industrial impetus, whilst an abundance of other natural resources ensured its rapid industrial growth.

Buying livestock is a serious business in Yorkshire, as is clear at one of the regular auctions held in Leyburn, North Yorkshire.

Autumn

THE CAPITAL IN AUTUMN

When the royal family leave behind them the chill of the Scottish Highlands after their annual visit to Balmoral, it is to return to the hazy autumn mists of London. A glance at the flagpole above the central

portico of Buckingham Palace will reveal whether Her Majesty the Queen, having returned from Scotland, is actually in residence. If the red and gold royal standard is flying, then she is there. A Buckingham House was built on the site in 1703 for the statesman John Sheffield (1648-1721), 1st Duke of Buckingham and Normanby. The house was bought by George III in 1761. George IV subsequently obtained from Parliament a grant for repairing, refurbishing and enlarging it, but, in concert with the architect John Nash (1752-1835), he decided to ignore the original

purposes of the grant and build something new. The building that Nash designed was in his usual grandiose style. Buckingham Palace, as it had become known, was still unfinished on George IV's death in 1830 and Nash, whose royal connections had not made him popular, was replaced as architect by Edward Blore (1787-1879). Blore promptly covered up Nash's work with a new facade. He also completely removed the massive marble arch that Nash had designed, on the instructions of George IV, in the style of the celebratory Arch of Constantine in Rome, as the gateway to the

Bicycle (top left), Underground (top right) and feet (above centre) are all vital modes of London transport! Above left: but the horses stand still on Horse Guards Parade. Above: a photographer employs some of the denizens of Trafalgar Square. In the background stands the statue of George IV and the National Gallery.

Palace. The arch was re-erected, in all its solitary splendour, at the northeast corner of Hyde Park, giving the name of Marble Arch to the point at which it stands. William IV disliked Buckingham Palace in spite of, or perhaps because of, the fact that he was born there and so it did not become a regular royal residence until the time of Queen Victoria. Her statue, designed by Sir Thomas Brock (1847-1922) as a part of her national memorial, stands in front of the Palace on an island around which taxi-drivers now delight in driving at great speed. The statue's surroundings were the work of Sir Aston Webb (1849-1930), who, as a further contribution to Victoria's memorial, designed Admiralty Arch at the end of the Mall leading into Trafalgar Square. He also laid out the Mall itself as a processional way, its glory spoiled more recently by the concrete box at the back of the Admiralty, built in

1940 as a bombproof shelter, which even an ivy covering cannot disguise. In 1913 Webb replaced the publicly visible eastern facade of Buckingham Palace, which had weathered badly, with the present one. The state rooms of the Palace are sumptuous, but the rest of the interior has the character of a large country house, comfortable, yet modest, and very quiet.

The church of St Martin-in-the-Fields existed in its present form long before Trafalgar Square, in which it stands, was built. William Hone (1780-1842), bookseller and journalist, records in his Table-Book

Top: standing guard, protected against the cold by a scarlet greatcoat. Buckingham Palace is protected by a high wall (left), decorated with ornamental urns on the south side. Feeding the pigeons in St James's Park (above) is more necessary in the colder months.

that 'vile houses' were being torn down in front of the church in 1826 to make way for the development of the square. So were the extensive royal stables, originally designed by William Kent (1684-1748), and the streets that served them, Great Mews, Green Mews and the appropriately-named Dunghill Mews. In their place rose the National Gallery, designed by William Wilkins (1778-1839) and erected in 1832-38, to house a complete collection of thirty-eight rare paintings and some other publicly-owned pictures. The former had been purchased by the Government in 1824 from the estate of John Julius Angerstein (d.1823), a wealthy merchant of Russian parentage, and the paintings

Left: the golden autumnal light surrounds a solitary walker in St James's Park. Below: trooping past Buckingham Palace and down Constitution Hill. A gentle stroll in Green Park (bottom) is the perfect antidote to busy city life.

included seven by Hogarth and also Titian's 'Venus and Adonis'. The gallery crowned the crest of the slope on which the new square had been constructed. Wilkins was hampered in that the government of the day altered the site for which his building had been designed and forced him to use some government surplus stock: the portico pillars once belonged to Carlton House, built for the then Prince Regent, later George IV, and demolished in 1829. An equestrian statue of George IV himself stands in Trafalgar Square in front of the gallery. Barefooted and wearing a toga, this representation of him was originally designed to go with the Marble Arch when that was to be the gateway to Buckingham Palace. Hence the Roman garb. Another statue in Trafalgar Square with a curious history is that of Charles I. This was originally commissioned by Sir Richard Weston (1577-1635), later 1st Earl of Portland, from Hubert Le Sueur (c.1595-c.1650), who presented a small model of it to Charles I himself. On the king's execution, the statue was sold for scrap to a brazier in Holborn, with orders

that it should be destroyed. The man kept it intact, however, and produced it on the Restoration of the Monarchy in 1660. He refused to surrender it to Weston's son and presented it instead to Charles II. It was re-erected near Charing Cross in 1674 on a pedestal designed by Grinling Gibbons (1648-1720) and sculpted in marble by Joshua Marshall (1629-1678). So Charles I, with his back to the National Gallery, gazes down Whitehall to the Houses of Parliament, where his execution was plotted, past the Banqueting House, before which the sentence of death was carried out in 1749. Dwarfing everything around is Nelson's Column, its foot guarded by a

Changing the guard at Buckingham Palace (far left) is best seen from a vantage point on the Victoria Memorial. The sickle belongs to the effigy of Agriculture. Left: Suffolk schoolgirls attending a service at St Martin-in-the-Fields. Below left: the news is no better secondhand. Below: an eye-catching window display is passed unnoticed. Bottom: a view down the Aldwych, on the edge of London's theatreland.

quartet of lions, each cast from a single original designed by Sir Edwin Landseer (1802-73), and by a permanent auxiliary detachment of fluttering pigeons. The Battle of Trafalgar and the death of Viscount Nelson, which the square commemorates, took place in 1805. The column, topped by its seventeen-foot-high statue, was not finished until 1843 and the lions did not take up their positions until 1867. This compares unfavourably with the speed with which the Scots put up their Nelson's Monument on Edinburgh's Calton Hill, which was in place in 1807.

Nelson's Column was designed to be a symbol of London for Londoners everywhere, as well as for visitors to the capital from other parts of Britain and from foreign countries. Like Big Ben, the Tower of London and St Paul's Cathedral, it has certainly become one. When it was first erected, without the lions, ordinary Londoners thought it was splendid. More learned observers were less impressed. They strongly deplored the design by William Railton (d. 1877), despite the fact that it had been selected after

two national competitions. Railton was an ecclesiastical architect who had visited the Mediterranean in 1825 and never quite recovered from the experience of seeing classical architecture in its context. For Nelson's Column, he imitated one of the Corinthian pillars of the Temple of Mars in the Forum of Rome, originally erected by the Emperor Augustus (63 B.C.-14 A.D.) to celebrate the vengeance he had wreaked on the murderers of Julius Caesar. The French philosopher, historian and critic Hippolyte Taine (1828-93) was equally scathing about the statue of Nelson surmounting the column, which he referred to in his *Notes on*

brother-in-law, Simon de Montfort (1208-65). This model parliament was the seed from which today's Parliament grew. When Parliament is sitting, a light shines from the top of the clock tower. The name Big Ben belongs not to the clock itself, nor even to the tower, but to the great bell inside it. It was named after the Commissioner of Works at the time of its casting in 1858, Sir Benjamin Hall (1802-67).

The Tower of London is down river from the Houses of Parliament. It is a magnificent, historic and, in some respects, horrific antiquity. As a Frenchman once remarked of it: 'The historical monuments of this

Tower Bridge (below) was built in 1894. Bottom left: waiting for a bus in New Oxford Street. The old red phone boxes (bottom right) are disappearing fast.

England (1872) as 'that hideous Nelson, stuck on his column with a coil of rope in the form of a pigtail, like a rat impaled on the top of a pole'. Trafalgar Square almost marks the easternmost point of the City of Westminster, chosen by Edward the Confessor, King of England from 1042 to 1066, as the site of his palace and of the great church which, as was customary, he ordered to be built beside it. The church was consecrated in December 1065, though it was still unfinished. Eight days later its originator was dead. In 1066, his successor, Harold, died at the battle of Hastings. William the Conqueror was duly crowned King in Westminster Abbey, as every English monarch has been since, excluding Edward V, who was murdered in the Tower of London in 1483, and Edward VIII, who abdicated in 1936. The present Westminster Abbey was built by Henry III in 1245, in the style of the great medieval churches of France. William the Conqueror had already rebuilt Edward's palace and added Westminster Hall. Here, in 1265, was held the first English parliament, forced upon Henry III by his

Left: all the fun of the fair in Leicester Square as Christmas draws near. The square takes its name from the Earls of Leicester, who had their London house on the north side of what was then called Leicester Fields. It was a resort of the fashionable in the eighteenth century, before becoming a haunt of hooligans and, in this century, a centre of entertainment.

earls and a former Lord Chancellor, Sir Thomas More, also lost their heads. Later victims of the axe were Archbishop Laud and the Duke of Monmouth, illegitimate son of Charles II. Famous prisoners have included not only the young Edward V and his brother, but also Elizabeth I, Sir Walter Raleigh, who wrote his *History of the World* whilst there, and Guy Fawkes. In 1666, the Great Fire of London started by Tower Bridge, on the opposite side of the river from the Tower. It swept away the original medieval and Tudor city of London and destroyed the old St Paul's Cathedral, designed by Inigo Jones (1573-1652) and finished only a few years before. The foundation stone of the replacement cathedral was laid in 1675 and Parliament finally declared it to be complete in 1711, by which time its architect, Sir Christopher Wren (1632-1723), was seventy-nine. A simple black stone marks his grave in the crypt, above which is the Latin inscription composed by his son: *Si monumentum requiris, circumspice,* 'If you want a memorial, look around you'.

Above: time to reflect in St Paul's Cathedral. In the cathedral crypt, which is said to be the largest in Europe, are the tombs of Lord Nelson and the Duke of Wellington, and also the grave of Sir Christopher Wren.

country, I notice, are popular in proportion to the horrors committed within their walls. Every self-respecting castle has a legend of bloodshed and murder.' In the case of the Tower, things perhaps got out of hand. This was especially true in the sixteenth century, when scores of heads rolled. They included those of two actual queens, Anne Boleyn and Catherine Howard, and one would-be queen, Lady Jane Grey, who was beheaded in the comparative privacy of Tower Green the same day that her husband met the same fate on Tower Hill, just outside the walls. Several

~ Britain and Her People ~

· CHAPTER 4 ·

WINTER

The English nature poet John Clare described the moment
when 'the cloudy days of autumn and of winter cometh on'.
In Scotland, the protection afforded by the curious land
formations can make it appear to be autumn in one place
(above) and bitter winter in another (right) at the same time.
Whichever it is, the Yorkshire miner (below) seems
cheerful enough.

THE VARSITY MATCH, TWICKENHAM

In the same way that 'The Boat Race' signifies the annual challenge match between the Oxford and Cambridge university rowing teams on the river Thames, so 'The Varsity Match' denotes the annual encounter between these two ancient institutions on the rugby football field. The first of these encounters took place in 1872. The Varsity Match is played at Twickenham, where a discreet Palladian mansion was once occupied by George II's mistress, the Countess of Suffolk, and later by Mrs Fitzherbert, George IV's secret wife. Now, soaring stands and broad terraces indicate that the former riverside resort is the home of English rugby football. The match traditionally takes place on the second Tuesday of December, just after the end of the university term. On that afternoon, to judge from the hordes of vociferous boys in school caps, from the armies of city gents in overcoats and suits, tweeds or blue blazers and from the numbers of clerical collars, all preparatory schools, all financial, industrial and agricultural institutions, all medical and legal practices and the Church of England shut up shop

in the south of England. The faithful travel by train from London's Waterloo Station and march in orderly columns along the suburban streets to the ground under the benevolent eye of cheerful policemen. They also come by car, manoeuvring their vehicles into suitable spots in the car park where they can serve as a base for a celebratory picnic lunch. There are a few wives and girlfriends, warmly wrapped in scarves and looking rather bemused, for this is a male-orientated occasion on which the Oxbridge rugby fraternity are reunited in a ritual celebration of their sport. For the spectators, the match is the most emotive and pulsating of all the annual sporting contests between the two rival universities and it certainly draws the greatest 'live' audience. For the players, it is an awe-inspiring occasion, though their first step into the arena from the players' tunnel is also cause for relief. The cachet

of a blue, the reward for being chosen to play in the Varsity Match, is only awarded to those who actually take the field. The disappointment of being selected and then being unable to play because of injury is one from which even the strongest and most eminent of men never recover, especially if that is their only chance of appearing in a match. Even those who have played in international matches for their country, in front of equally large crowds, before going to Oxford or Cambridge, find the atmosphere positively fearsome. With the increase in international fixtures and tours, the sheer competitiveness of modern club rugby and the fitness required of its players, the Varsity Match has ceased to be the showpiece of the game that it once was. Nevertheless, the occasion, with its unique blend of companionship and partisanship, retains all its fervour.

The spectators of the Varsity Match are drawn from all age groups. It is an annual mecca for prep school boys and City businessmen, as well as Oxbridge undergraduates, each without exception an enthusiastic partisan. Like so many British sporting occasions, it seems a justification for people to gather as much in the cause of eating and drinking as to watch the game. However, the vast Twickenham ground is packed for the game itself, which is played in an appropriately enthusiastic manner. Above: members of a London club relax before joining the pilgrimage to Twickenham. The mural records a famous 'streaking' incident on a different Twickenham occasion.

Winter

GRASSINGTON – A VILLAGE CELEBRATES

Grassington, situated in the Yorkshire Dales National Park, is classified as a village, yet is livelier and contains more of interest than many towns several times its size. The capital of upper Wharfedale, it contains the remains of an Iron Age fort and village. It stands at the point where two important medieval routes, the monastic road from Fountains Abbey to the Lake District and the agricultural road from Skipton to Wensleydale, crossed. In 1281, by a royal charter of Edward I, a weekly market was established in the village. James I brought in men from Derbyshire to mine lead ore from Grassington Moor. In later years, there was a flourishing textile industry in the village.

Part of the Old Hall was built in the thirteenth century. The bridge over the River Wharfe dates from 1603 and many of the cottages were also built around that time. There is a steep main street and a cobbled square and many of the streets and alleys have unusual names, such as Chamber End Fold, Jakey and The Woggins. The Grassington Players perform in a theatre created by the postmaster in the early nineteenth

century in a converted barn. The Grassington stage was once trodden by the tragedian Edmund Kean (1787-1833) and by the actress Harriott Mellon (1777-1837), at her best as the impertinent chambermaid in comedies of the time.

By long tradition, the Grassington Feast takes place every year in October, reflecting the Michaelmas Feast of medieval times. A much more recent tradition, dating from 1982, has inspired a unique annual celebration of the works and person of the English novelist Charles Dickens (1812-70). This rather bizarre but colourful and enjoyable occasion is a blend of

literary make-believe, Christian tradition, folklore and rustic rites. It also attracts visitors and tourists. The event is staged with the enthusiastic cooperation of the villagers and their costumiers and seamstresses. Anybody walking into the grocer's, the butcher's, the craft shop or the pub will be greeted and served by an early Victorian reincarnation. Victorian urchins, their faces suitably dirtied, dart around the streets. Visitors can spot Little Nell, Nicholas Nickleby, Betsey Trotwood and even Mr Pickwick himself! The Grassington Players act out, in the open air, a local version of the story of St George and the Dragon, in which Father Christmas

When Grassington stages its annual Dickens festival, all the village gets involved. Whole families dress up and the shopkeepers turn Victorian, even if their goods remain firmly twentieth century. Amongst the faces are some recognisable Dickens characters.

plays a part. The children perform their nativity play. At night, Morris dancers, their noses blue with cold, cut their jolly capers, before retiring thankfully to the warmth of the pub, where they make more music.

Charles Dickens, the subject of all this celebration, was born not in Yorkshire, but in Portsmouth. He was the second of eight children of a Navy pay clerk whose efforts to maintain a suitable lifestyle for his family culminated in his imprisonment for debt. The novelist moved home fourteen times in as many years and spent several months working in a blacking warehouse. He started work as a solicitor's clerk in 1827 and two years later, having learned shorthand, he became a

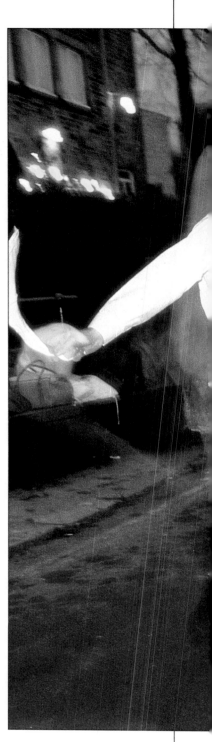

newspaper reporter. He thought about going on the stage and applied to Covent Garden Theatre for an audition, which he missed through illness. He abandoned the idea when his first story was published in 1833. *The Posthumous Papers of the Pickwick Club* began serialisation in March 1836, a few days before his marriage to Catherine Hogarth. Her seventeen-year-old sister Mary came to live with them. Mary's sudden death a year later, literally in Dickens' arms, proved traumatic and she became for him a perpetual embodiment of youth and innocence. It also caused him to suspend the writing of *Oliver Twist* for a month. His career became an incessant round of

Top left: a shop in which the Victorians would have felt very much at home. Top centre: Victorian urchins warm themselves in traditional outdoor fashion. 'It's my opinion, sir, that this meeting is drunk, sir!' (Pickwick Papers). Behind the bar of a local inn (above left), they're ready for anything. Below left: as night falls, the actors in the play join the procession.

writing, punctuated by frequent fact-finding, publicity or family tours that was only halted in 1870 by his death from a cerebral haemorrhage after finishing six instalments of *The Mystery of Edwin Drood*. In 1853 he gave a public reading of his works, for charity. The response was such that in 1858 he started doing it on a regular basis, for himself. Essentially, Dickens was a comic writer of genius with a gift for characterisation and a highly-developed sense of drama. He also used the social conditions of the time, of which he was an indefatigable observer, to enhance the effect of his stories. It was as an observer that he travelled to Yorkshire in early 1838 to investigate reports of brutality in boarding schools for orphaned boys. He began to write *The Life and Adventures of Nicholas Nickleby* as soon as he got back to London and the first episode was published on 31 March 1838. The novel's Dotheboys Hall is the archetype of these notorious schools, but the original is said to have been the one run by William Shaw at Bowes, which is some miles to the north of Grassington. The school was forced to close after publication began, but the building survives.

Top: the Morris dancers cut a caper on the village street. 'I live on broken wittles – and I sleep on the coals', was the complaint of the waiter in David Copperfield. The waiter's lot is much cosier in Grassington (left). Above: the Artful Dodger?

Winter

HM PRISON, DARTMOOR

In 1988, the eighty-five prisons of England and Wales housed nearly 48,000 inmates, the largest prison population of any country in Europe. Scotland has a separate system. Many prisoners, moreover, are crammed into Victorian buildings that were certainly not intended to serve until the end of the following century! Dartmoor is the oldest prison still in use and is set square in the bleakest expanse of land in the south of England. It was originally the idea of Sir Thomas Tyrwhitt, Lord Warden of the Stannaries, the ancient court that had jurisdiction over the tin miners of Devon and Cornwall. In an effort to develop the amenities of Dartmoor, he built himself a magnificent mansion in the middle of it in 1785-98. When he had problems finding labour to extend his scheme, he drafted in French prisoners from the Napoleonic wars. The prison was built between 1806 and 1813 to accommodate this work force. In 1850 it was enlarged for use as a civil prison. Charles Dickens, a noted student of social conditions, may well have visited it in the course of his investigations, just as he inspected

jails in America during a six-month tour with his wife in 1842. 'The Moor', as it is uncompromisingly known, symbolises all that is harshest in the British penal system. There is some justification for this view. Until twenty years ago, Dartmoor housed the most hardened criminals. Although its inmates now represent the more run-of-the-mill wrongdoer and each man has an eight-foot by four-foot cell to himself, the dreadful cold and damp still permeate everything. Sir Herbert Samuel, Home Secretary in 1931-32 and a philosopher as well as a politician, remarked after a visit: 'I would call it a cauldron of vice if it were not so damned cold'. According to an authorised report, the heating system is in use even in summer, to dry out dripping walls and saturated bedding. The comparative attraction of a single cell and room service for meals is diminished if breakfast, lunch and tea, having been wheeled across a courtyard and delivered in containers to each wing of the prison, are solitary affairs, eaten in locked cells. There is now a more liberal attitude to recreational facilities in the prison, and home leave and visiting regulations are stretched for families who have travelled long distances. The biggest social problem, which is being tackled by means of a 'pre-release course', is how prisoners will adjust to the very different kind of bleakness they will find outside the prison's walls.

Facing page and top right: barred gates and metal grilles, potent symbols of incarceration. That traditional prison occupation, sewing mail-bags (top left), still survives. Meals are delivered (above centre), but company is limited (above). Above left: forestry work on the moors for prisoners shortly to be released.

Winter

ROYAL NAVAL COLLEGE, DARTMOUTH

As an alternative to prison, criminals in the eighteenth century might be sentenced to 'the hulks', disused wooden warships or merchant vessels called back into service as jails. Not so many miles from Dartmoor Prison, at the mouth of the River Dart, stands a different sort of institution whose inmates were, until 1905, confined in hulks. In the Middle Ages, Dartmouth itself was one of Devon's, and England's, chief seaports. It was here that Richard I, nicknamed the Lionheart, assembled his fleet in 1190 for the third crusade. In 1346 the port raised thirty-one ships to besiege Calais, a number exceeded only by Fowey and Yarmouth. Yet, in spite being a leader in the Newfoundland fishing trade, Dartmouth's fortunes declined until, in 1863, it was selected as the site of a new training establishment for officer cadets in the Royal Navy.

The British Navy has a history which goes back to King Alfred the Great (849-99), who ordered his subjects living on the coast of Wessex to build a fleet of warships, with which he seriously discomfited the

Danes who had been occupying the northern and midland regions of England for ten years. King Edward the Confessor (c.1003-66) made the mistake of disbanding, for reasons of political expediency, the permanent fleet which his predecessors had maintained out of taxes, as a result of which King Harold (c.1022-66) had only a scratch force with which to oppose the landing of William the Conqueror. The translation of the 'king's ships' into a nationally administered naval force began with Henry VIII (1491-1547), who set up a forerunner of the Board of Admiralty. The Navy became the Royal Navy in the time of Charles II (1630-

85), but it was under his brother James, Duke of York (1633-1701), later James II, and the hard-working Secretary to the Admiralty and famous diarist, Samuel Pepys (1633-1703), that a far-reaching administration was established. The Admiralty was reorganised in 1832 by the then First Lord, Sir James Graham (1792-1861). The post of First Lord of the Admiralty was a political one. He was assisted by several Sea Lords, the First Sea Lord being responsible for the mobilisation and fitness of the fleet and for the selection of its senior officers. It was under this system that the Royal Naval College was founded.

Facing page: saluting the colour from the ramps at the front of the College. Learning to march (top left) is just as important as more academic study (top right). Centre: the students' view of the College during morning Divisions. More practical dress (above left) is required for manoeuvres, at the end of which the craft must always be hosed down (above).

The first Dartmouth cadets were housed in a three-decker sailing ship-of-the-line, *Britannia*, which was joined the following year by HMS *Hindostan*. By 1869 the original hulk had been pronounced too small for its purpose and was replaced by a bigger wooden ship, HMS *Prince of Wales*, which was renamed *Britannia*. It was not until 1896 that anyone saw the need for a permanent building on dry land. The Britannia Royal Naval College was formally opened by Edward VII in 1905. The impressive structure of stone and red brick, with its towers and pinnacles, was designed by Sir Aston Webb (1849-1930).

It was a time of expansion and change in the Navy. In 1897 Rear Admiral, later Grand Admiral, Alfred

von Tirpitz (1849-1930) became Secretary of State for the German Navy and shortly afterwards he presented to the Reichstag his first Navy Bill. A second bill, brought in in 1900, effectively began the naval arms race. Tirpitz's counterpart in Britain at this time was William Waldegrave Palmer (1859-1942), 2nd Earl of Selborne, who was First Lord of the Admiralty from 1900 to 1905. A man of foresight and courage, he was instrumental in pushing through the appointment as Second Sea Lord in 1902 of Sir, later Lord, John Fisher (1841-1920), as a means of

promulgating his plans for a more realistic system of training and education for the Royal Navy. As First Sea Lord from 1904 to 1910, Fisher revitalised and redeployed the Navy. The syllabus which was introduced at Dartmouth to mark the opening of the new college buildings and which was far ahead of its time in its scope and in its combination of scientific and technical subjects, was devised by Fisher but named after Lord Selborne, who had cleared the way for its adoption.

Originally, cadets entered the college at the age of thirteen, but the age was raised in 1948 to sixteen.

Top left: keeping a sharp lookout when leaving the quay. Top: it's hats off for prayers. Above left: the naval leaders of the future are overlooked in the Senior Gunroom by famous figures from the past. A sextant (above) is just one of the pieces of equipment cadets must learn to use.

Above: the early morning winter sun illuminates the ramps and impressive facade of the college. Officer cadets in the Women's Royal Naval Service also train at Britannia Royal Naval College. Left: 'eyes right' during a march past. Parade ground training instils discipline, encourages personal smartness and increases self-confidence.

Since 1955 the ages of Officers Under Training, no longer called cadets, at the college has ranged from seventeen to thirty-five. All branches of the force are represented. These include WRNS officer cadets, midshipmen who joined the navy straight from school and university graduates who, as sub-lieutenants, enter one of the main specialisations of seaman, engineer, supply and secretariat or instructor. Direct entry officers, such as doctors, dentists, instructors, chaplains and nursing officers, spend a short time at the college to accustom themselves to naval life.

The training at Dartmouth is as much about leadership as about academic and physical ability or practical skills. Having been accepted for the course by the Admiralty Interview Board, new entry midshipmen are put through their paces almost immediately on arrival at Dartmouth. During their first week, they are sent up river in picket boats and put ashore to complete a three-hour night march, before returning to the boats for the night. The next morning, there is a five-hour hike, after which the boats return down river and put out to sea for combined manoeuvres. All this is only a part of the exercise. No leaders are appointed – it is each man for himself, with a difference. A watch

Below left: the Captain and some of the crew of HMS Peterel which, together with HMS Sandpiper (left) is part of the Dartmouth Navigational Training Squadron. Below: Ceremonial Divisions, for which the whole college is on parade.

Far left: at ease before Britannia, cadets await their inspecting officer. Above: the Colour Sergeant ensures all is present and correct on the parade ground. The atmosphere is more relaxed in the Senior Gunroom (left) at lunchtime. Training makes for hearty appetites and the food has to be substantial to satisfy them. Facing page: ready to raise the Ensign.

is being kept for those who show initiative, have confidence in their own abilities and are not afraid to give orders to their peers. The first half term culminates in a three-day exercise on Dartmoor, living outdoors whatever the weather, which can be positively foul! This is a test of leadership and teamwork, as well as of endurance. The second term is spent at sea in the Dartmouth training ship, an assignment which involves menial labour alongside the ordinary seamen, practical training in seamanship and a taste of foreign travel. There are special privileges for those in their final two terms. They may use the Senior Gunroom for socialising and sleep in single cabins. They also wear white, instead of blue, shirts and play a part in the day-to-day administration of their particular division. In addition, each is expected to act as a 'guide, philosopher and friend' to a new entrant, to learn the qualities required of a naval officer in caring for his men's interests at sea.

Winter

CATS

The Egyptians had a cat goddess called Bast, whose centre of worship was at Bubastis. Here, according to the Greek historian Herodotus (c.480-c.425 B.C.), once a year vast numbers of devotees crammed into boats, playing pipes, clashing cymbals, singing and clapping their hands, the men making rude remarks and lewd gestures to any women they passed on the banks of the river. He goes on to say that 700,000 people attended the festival, in the course of which more wine was drunk than during the whole of the rest of the year. Diodorus, a Sicilian historian, who lived in the first century B.C., reported that anyone killing a cat in Egypt, even accidentally, was put to death, if they

the fact that 'by stroking of him I have found out electricity'. Cats really came into their own in Victorian times. The first cat show in Britain was held in 1871 at the Crystal Palace. The National Cat Club was founded in 1887 and has held its own show almost every year since then. In modern times, Stevie Smith (1902-71) has written poems about cats, including one she saw with its mistress on the London Underground. So has T.S. Eliot (1888-1965), in a rather lighter and more satirical vein. Cats are not gregarious, as Rudyard Kipling (1865-1936) pointed out with much wisdom in his story, *The Cat that Walked by Himself*, from the *Just So Stories*. They are also utterly inscrutable,

had not already been lynched by the mob. There are hardly any references to cats as pets in Greek or Roman literature, though their images appear on vases or in mosaics. They were, however, widely kept in China from about 500 A.D. and begin to appear in European literature during the Middle Ages. Geoffrey Chaucer (c.1343-1400) describes in *The Canterbury Tales* a cat which, however pampered, will abandon 'every dainty in the house' to pursue a mouse. There are many passing references to cats in the plays of William Shakespeare (1564-1616), whilst the Scottish poet William Drummond of Hawthornden (1585-1649) wrote a poem in which he laments that 'with a traitrous leap' a cat has surprised and killed a pet sparrow. For the first genuine cat study, however, one needs to read the lines in *Jubilate Agno* by Christopher Smart (1722-71), who developed religious mania in his thirties and spent many years in asylums. He was obviously devoted to his cat, who was called Jeoffry, and minutely describes him performing a ten-part ritual before going off in search of food and delights in

as was discovered by the French philosopher and essayist, Michel de Montaigne (1533-92): 'When I play with my cat, who knows whether she isn't amusing herself with me more than I am with her'.

Judges, stewards, exhibitors and exhibits at the National Cat Club Show held annually at Olympia. Over 2,500 cats, each one its owner's pride and joy, are on show at the event, which draws 15,000 visitors. Cats and owners are often equally glamorous and certainly equally well groomed. The show is living proof of the British love of animals.

Winter

THE FESTIVE SEASON, LONDON

'There is no more dangerous or disgusting habit than that of celebrating Christmas before it comes,' wrote G.K. Chesterton (1874-1936), journalist, poet and creator of that most amiable of detectives, Father Brown. Yet shopkeepers in London's West End wait impatiently for the day when the decorative lights of Regent Street are formally switched on. This ceremony has little to do with the celebration of Christmas and a lot to do with the tradition of consumer spending and self-indulgence at this time of the year. When, as happened one year, a popular television and pop star from down under, who had been invited to perform this onerous task, had to delay her appearance, there were loud complaints that business was being lost by such presumption. It is as though throwing the switch electrifies the Christmas shoppers as well as the elaborate, illuminated decorations that dangle across the street and climb up the buildings. As moths are drawn to a candle, so people flock to the lights and, having wondered at them, pour into the elite of the capital's specialist and department stores and then fight their way home with bursting shopping bags.

In Regent Street you can also visit Hamley's, the biggest toy shop in London, if not in the whole of

Chauffered limousine (top left) may be the best way to go Christmas shopping when it's raining, but most shoppers have to rely on buses (left). Some lights are perennial (above centre), but they're no match for the Christmas lights in Regent Street (facing page), where carols (top right) maintain shoppers' spirits. Roast chestnuts (above) are another seasonal treat. Streets littered with rubbish (far left) are anything but.

Britain, and watch fathers playing with the mechanical toys. Those who have been sufficiently strong-minded not to have overburdened themselves with parcels may pause at the bottom end of the street and consider Piccadilly Circus, which a Frenchman once dubbed 'the navel of London'. Eros can usually be seen, standing permanently on one foot atop the fountain, but the base of the statue may be shrouded against revellers in protective, yet tastefully decorated, boards. The statue is not actually Eros at all, in that the figure does not represent the mischievous winged archer of Greek myth, but is *The Angel of Christian Charity*, sculpted by Sir Alfred Gilbert (1854-1934) as a memorial to the 7th Earl of Shaftesbury (1801-85), the Victorian philanthropist. Although the statue is constant, in other respects Picadilly Circus shows continuous evidence of reconstruction and change. The department store whose main door onto the circus was once a traditional place to meet one's partner, the great cinema with its Art-Deco frontage, the vast teahouse where one could sit and watch other shoppers struggle by, and a favourite nightspot of the middle classes have all ceased to exist. Shaftesbury Avenue strikes out northwards from Piccadilly Circus, joining Charing Cross Road and forming, with Regent Street and Oxford Street, the rough boundaries of the area known as Soho. Soho is trying to rehabilitate itself by playing up its reputation as a centre *par excellence* for fine and exotic restaurants and delicatessens and for congenial pubs and by playing down the sleazier elements of its past, which have brought the area a different kind of popularity and repute.

The Christmas spirit invades Regent Street (above left), but cannot save even a Rolls Royce from the unwelcome embrace of a wheel clamp (above). Nothing is above London's parking laws.

Winter

A HARRODS' CHRISTMAS

Harrods, arguably the most famous department store in the world, aims to fulfil its Latin motto *Omnia, omnibus, ubique*, 'Everything, for everyone, everywhere'. The store was established in 1849 when Henry Charles Harrod bought a small grocery shop from a friend. It has been growing and increasing in showmanship ever since. Today, it has an average of 50,000 patrons a day and forty per cent of its sales are to overseas customers, whose orders have included six

bread rolls to go to an address in New York, a refrigerator to go to Finland and a Persian carpet to Iran. Not only can you buy anything from an *objet d'art* to a pet, from a sauna bath to a piece of cheese, or from a satellite-receiving dish to a handkerchief within its walls, but the store runs its own bank, funeral service, kennels, tourist information desk, dry cleaners, hairdressing and beauty salons and circulating library. There are also seven restaurants, three bars, a pub, a coffee shop and a health juice bar. At Christmas and during the sales in January and July, the staff of 4,000, of whom half are on the sales side, rises to 6,000. The distinctive facade was completed in 1905, but the interior has been taken apart and remodelled many times and now incorporates a waterfall.

The world-famous facade, with its beautifully dressed windows, and the equally elaborate Food Hall are important parts of the tourist attraction that is Harrods. Christmas time simply adds to those attractions with seasonal merchandise and glittering decorations, and carol singers enhance the scene. Outside is a memorial (left) to Harrods' saddest day, 17 December 1983, when an IRA car bomb killed six people and wounded 93.

Winter

CHRISTMAS EVE, GLOUCESTER

Gloucester Cathedral looks much as it did in about 1490, although it was not a cathedral until 1541, but a Benedictine abbey. Parts of it, notably the nave, the crypt under the chancel, part of the chancel itself and the overall ground plan go back to 1090, whilst the glorious Perpendicular tower dates from about 1450. The design was innovative in that the Norman arcades of the nave consist of massive, plain circular piers that rise to a great height and are then surmounted by markedly narrow arches. The huge window in the east wall of the choir is the largest in England to have stone

tracery. Much of the glass is original and commemorates the dead of the battle of Crécy in 1346 and others who died in the Hundred Years War, some of whose heraldic devices are incorporated in the design. In 1337 the Abbot of Gloucester accepted for burial the remains of the murdered Edward II. His royal tomb, with its idealised alabaster effigy symbolising kingship, under an elaborate canopy, is a very fine example of medieval funerary art. It was largely because of the presence of these royal remains and the veneration of Edward as a saint that it was possible for the eastern part of the church to be reconstructed in its present form. Among the cathedral's chief glories are the adjoining cloisters of the monastic quarters, which were rebuilt in the fourteenth century and provided little carrels on the south side in which the monks could pursue their studies. Christmas Eve is celebrated with two family services, during which the choristers process, sing and light candles on three Christmas trees in the cathedral. Gloucester is noted for its choir and, with Hereford and Worcester, makes up the trio of cathedrals that takes turns to host the annual Three Choirs Festival in September. Instituted in 1724, this features contemporary choral works as well as such popular oratorios as *The Messiah* and *Elijah*.

Having rehearsed (top left) and then let off steam (left) before the service, the choir gather (above centre) and process into the cathedral (top right) together with members of the clergy (above) and all due pomp and ceremony. Facing page: as the procession comes up the Norman aisle, the choristers begin to take their seats at each side of the choir. Above far left: the choir gather before the Christmas tree to sing.

Winter

A BOXING DAY'S HUNT

''Unting,' explained Mr Jorrocks, 'is all that's worth living for – all time is lost wot is not spent in 'unting – it is like the hair we breathe – if we have it not we die – it's the sport of kings, the image of war without its guilt, and only five-and-twenty per cent of its danger.' Mr Jorrocks was the creation of Robert Smith Surtees (1803-64), journalist, novelist and, when he inherited his father's house and estate in County Durham in

1838, country gentleman. He was the first novelist to write about fox-hunting and he did so with much verve, realism and social satire. The hunting season starts in November, by which time the young hounds will have learned their business. The hunt will set out at about eleven in the morning, when the fox, if there is one, will have returned to his lair after the night's foray. Once he has been disturbed and has broken away from his covert, he is allowed to travel some way before the alarm is raised, to avoid his returning to his base. What actually governs the scent and its nature is as little understood today as it was in the time of Mr Jorrocks.

That hunting is a sport for all is as dubious an assertion as that it is an environmentally desirable

The traditional stirrup cup, likely these days to be just a sherry to accompany a piece of cake, warms the huntsmen before they set off. The crowds that have gathered to see them off must make do with warm clothing. Regulation dress ensures the huntsman also stays warm and comfortable throughout the day.

Left: the North Cotswold Hunt sets off, watched with interest (far left). Then it's a case of milling around (below) until the direction is given (bottom).

pastime. A horse, whether owned or borrowed, is the most obvious and expensive necessity. The velvety covering of a riding hat only marginally conceals the fact that it is actually a crash helmet and must stay firmly in place at all times and under all circumstances, most especially when the wearer is about to land upon it. The carefully tied and knotted stock is not for show either. It is to support the neck in case of a fall. Most hunt followers wear black coats, cut to fit, thick and well-lined, for it can be bitterly cold galloping over those expanses of open country. Regular followers of, and subscribers to, the hunt may be awarded the equivalent of their first eleven colours by the Master and thus qualify to wear a red coat. This is definitely red, not pink, nor is it called 'pink'. In hunting circles pink is an adjunct only of gin. Traditionally, hunting coats are not dry-cleaned after a hard day in the field, but steeped in several changes of pure rain water and then hung up to dry. Breeches may be white and tight, or twill and loose. Rubber boots are infra dig, clammy and poor protection. The proper wear is leather boots, honed to a parade-ground shine using polish, elbow grease and frequent 'boning'. Black boots are worn with black coats and black with brown tops with red coats. Spurs may be worn, but are mainly for show. The curious attraction of fox-hunting was summed up

by Siegfried Sassoon (1886-1967), an avid fan of Surtees, in his description of a young man's first outing: 'For no apparent reason the people around me suddenly set off at a gallop and for several minutes I was aware of nothing but the breathless flurry of being carried along, plentifully spattered with mud by the sportsman in front of me. Suddenly, without any warning, he pulled up. [My horse] automatically followed suit, shooting me well up her neck. The next moment everyone turned round and we all went tearing back by the way we had come'.

Facing page: what the well-dressed huntsman is wearing. The garter is purely decorative and the crop is nominally for controlling the hounds. The flask, however, has a very practical purpose.

Winter

RINGING IN THE NEW YEAR

Nothing in the recent past has caused such social divisiveness between England and Scotland as the way in which their respective countrymen have celebrated the yuletide holiday. Within living memory, Christmas Day was not a holiday in Scotland and men and women went to work as usual, conserving their energies for New Year's Eve, or Hogmanay. This was a perfectly acceptable arrangement as long as each nation observed its own customs in its own country. However, when the Scots in England began to regard 1 January as a holiday anyway, either to recover from the excesses of the previous night or to disappear back home to celebrate, something had to be done. So now the English and the Scots have both 25 December and 1 January as public holidays, often taking the days between as holiday, too. It is only the Scots, however, who retain any ritual observance of the new year.

New Year's Day itself is an arbitrary date which differs among various peoples and countries and may even be celebrated on different days by separate communities within a single country. In the Jewish

calendar, new year celebrations began as an extension of the festivities accompanying the final gathering in of the harvest. It was then decided that the religious year should begin with a period of reflection and that a penitential period should precede the celebration. Its beginning is the first day of the seventh month of the Jewish calendar, the month of Tishri, which day is also regarded as the anniversary of the creation of the world and as the Day of Judgement. Practically every city in ancient Greece had its own calendar, but the civil year usually began with the first new moon after the summer solstice and was thus generally in July.

The original Roman year began on 15 March, a sensible date in that it reflects the onset of spring and of new growth. 1 January was established as the first day of the Roman year, and subsequently of the Christian year, as a matter of sheer political and administrative convenience. In 153 B.C., to enable the incoming consul's arrival in Spain to coincide with the beginning of the campaign season, the beginning of his year of office, and thus of the year itself, was advanced to 1 January and there it has remained. The reformed calendar which Julius Caesar instituted in about 45 B.C., on the advice of a peripatetic

A good-natured, boisterous jollity has come to typify the traditional New Year celebrations in London's Trafalgar Square.

Alexandrian astronomer called Sosigenes, enabled the traditional agricultural year, based on the circuit of the earth round the sun, to be reconciled with the duration of a complete revolution of the moon round the earth. His year of 365 days, 366 every fourth year, was actually eleven minutes and fourteen seconds out and remained so until the sixteenth century, when Pope Gregory corrected the error. Those who stick to the old calendar celebrate New Year's Day on 13 January. On New Year's Day, the Romans gave gifts, which were known as *strenae*, from which comes the French term for New Year's Day, *le jour d'étrennes*. The custom of giving gifts on New Year's Day also existed

Far left: for some, the party spirit is just all too much. Left: high jinks played out with the floodlit steeple of St Martin-in-the-Fields in the background. The Christmas tree (below) is an anuual gift from Norway.

Left: the crowd and its uniformed minders mill around in silence, waiting for the clocks to strike midnight and the bells to ring the New Year in.

in England up until the time of Charles II. Earlier, this tradition had begun to get out of hand in that this was also the day on which magistrates accepted bribes, a custom which was, however, abolished by law in 1290. In Scotland in early Celtic times, New Year's Day was on 1 November. In Christian times, up until 1600, it was on 25 March. In 1600, the change of date to 1 January brought New Year's Day within the twelve-day celebration of Yule, and when the celebration of Christmas and of its subsidiary festival, Twelfth Night, were banned at the time of the Reformation, the junketings and some of the traditions associated with

them were transferred to New Year's Eve. Hogmanay is a time of good will, and kissing 'for luck' has a long tradition in Scotland. So has the Het Pint, a formidable wassail consisting of hot ale, spiced with nutmeg and laced with whisky, and the Hogmanay Black Bun. Many Scottish households still observe the custom of first-footing, welcoming the first person, and those following, other than a member of the household, to enter their home after midnight. For the most propitious results, the first-footer should be a dark-haired man, bearing as gifts a piece of coal, symbolising fuel, a slice of black bun or shortbread and a bottle of whisky!

Winter

COAL – NORTH YORKSHIRE

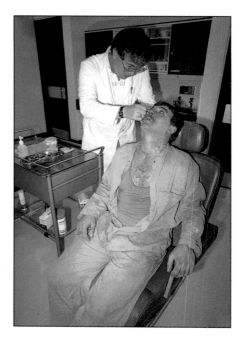

The piece of coal that the Scottish first-footer brings into the home on New Year's Day to represent fuel is also the symbol of a British industry which goes back at least to the twelfth century and probably very much earlier – the Romans certainly had a word for coal. The monks of Kirkstall Abbey, who were apparently in the iron forging business, were allowed to dig for coal in 1161 and there are records of other coal mining operations in Yorkshire at around the same time, notably at Pontefract and Hipperholme. Today, the hundred or so collieries in Britain are divided for control purposes into eight areas, of which the North Yorkshire Area contains eighteen collieries. Coal mining played a vital role in the industrial revolution of the eighteenth and nineteenth centuries. In the peak year of 1913 the industry produced 292,000,000 tonnes of coal, of which 74,200,000 tonnes were exported. In 1986-87 the output was just 106,900,000 tonnes, but against this must be set the fact that total consumption within Britain over that year was 113,100,000 tonnes, seventy per cent of which was

used by power stations. The North Yorkshire Area employs about 18,000 people, of whom about two thirds are actually involved in extracting the coal, and it has a turnover of some £700,000,000 a year. About eighty-four per cent of the output goes towards generating electricity and only two per cent finds its way into domestic use. Denby Grange, near Wakefield, was first sunk in 1791 and is the oldest pit in the whole of Yorkshire. Other North Yorkshire pits that were sunk in the nineteenth century and are still operating are Allerton Bywater (1875), Houghton/Darfield, comprising two mines originally opened in 1860 and

1873 respectively, Park Mill (1880) and Prince of Wales (1875). At the other end of the scale, there are five mines that only came into being in the 1980s which make up the Selby complex and are linked together underground. Huge conveyors at Gascoigne Wood are designed to bring the output of all five to the surface, from where it is despatched to the nearby power station at Drax. The British coal industry is one of the most technologically advanced in the world. The modern miner may still have coal dust on his face, but today he is more of a technician, operating machinery developed for an age that still requires coal as fuel.

Top left and above left: waiting to go down at Ricall Colliery. It's not difficult to spot those whose shift has just finished (above centre left and facing page). Above centre: eye inspection at the infirmary. Above: a shift superintendent at Gascoigne Wood.

Winter

VALLEYS OF THE MINERS

Of all the towns in the industrial valleys of south Wales, Merthyr Tydfil is regarded as the archetype. In the middle of the eighteenth century it was a quiet market town supporting ninety-three farms that served a wide area with their products. Merthyr was also noted for its auctioneers, as one might expect of an agricultural centre, and for its clock-makers, which one would not expect. By 1801 the town had become the most populous place in Wales and it remained so for sixty years. Four great ironworks, Cyfarthfa, Dowlais, Penydarren and Plymouth, brought workers crowding in from England as well as from all over Wales. Their appalling working conditions meant that the average life expectancy of a working man in Merthyr in 1850 was seventeen years and even for tradesmen it was only thirty-two. Industrial unrest was a continuing

feature throughout the century; riots were commonplace. When the Depression began to bite in Britain in the 1920s, Merthyr was already suffering from the effects of changes in the use of fuel and in methods of steel production. By the 1930s, it had been classified as a Distressed Area. On Sunday, 3

Top left: the grim aspect of Ogmore Vale. Port Talbot (top right and left) is a coal port and steel town. Above far left: children play outside the long terraces of houses at Blaengarw (far left). Above: terraced houses line up across a hillside at New Tredegar.

February, 1935 the valleys came alive. Three hundred thousand people, equivalent to a seventh of the entire population of Wales, marched in protest against their treatment at the hands of the Government. The next day, the women of Merthyr had their say. They marched to the offices of the Unemployment Assistance Board and tore the place apart. Other demonstrations followed, as a direct result of which the Government's unpopular new relief regulations were shelved for eighteen months. This was a morale booster for the people of Wales, but it did not actually alleviate conditions in the valleys. In 1939, the commissioners reported that half the adult male population of the Dowlais area was surplus to the requirements of local industries and services. In Merthyr itself, seventy per cent were unemployed and the organisation called Political and Economic Planning proposed that the

town be abandoned and its population sent to the Wye Valley in the west of England. The Second World War offered only an illusory respite. Between June 1980 and June 1982 the working population of Wales fell by ten per cent. That figure taken on its own conceals the fact that the steel industry shed half its work force at a time when coal mines were also being shut down. There is still a coal industry in the valleys and Wales accounts for about one third of Britain's steel production, but the area is one of the poorest in the country. It is as though, when the valleys lost so many of their people through emigration, they lost their heart as well.

Top: the Afan valley. Left: a child playing in Merthyr Tydfil, her surroundings typical of the area in general. Above: a solitary figure ventures down the street in Blaengarw.

Winter

A SOUTH WALES WEDDING

There is nothing new about equal rights for women in Wales. In Celtic times, they were respected in ways for which their sisters elsewhere, and later Welsh women, have had to fight. Indeed, the principle behind a wife's entitlement to a down payment if the couple separated within seven years of the marriage and to half the husband's property after seven years has only been recently re-accepted. In the Middle Ages, there was a custom in Wales that predates the American 'shower' by several centuries. People were bidden to attend a gathering at an inn to 'launch' a betrothed couple. In the seventeenth century, there still survived a tradition that may have had its roots in heroic legend. On the wedding day, the groom and his supporters rode to the bride's house and demanded her surrender. When the groom was given the statutory refusal, there was a

mock battle, during which the bride would flee on horseback with her nearest male relative, hotly pursued by the groom. She was always caught.

The custom of 'bundling', that is courting in bed, was still rife in Wales as late as the mid-nineteenth century. 'I have had the greatest difficulty in keeping my servants from practising it,' complained a vicar. 'It became necessary to secure their chamber windows with bars to prevent them from admitting men. I am told by my parishioners that unless I allow the practice, I shall very soon have no servants at all and that it will be impossible to get any.' There were, however, rules that applied when bundling took place in the girl's parents' house. The lovers were expected to retain some if not all of their clothing, and a bolster might well be placed strategically between them. Like many customs, this one was based on common sense. In winter, when it was too cold to court outside and fuel might be in short supply, bed was the most comfortable place for a conversation. Bundling was thus a pastime of reason and not the early onset of the permissive age.

Pre-wedding gatherings and post-wedding groupings at Old Cwmbran, Gwent. Facing page: the teenage bride and bridegroom line up with some of their wedding guests.

Winter

THE COAST IN WINTER

The reason why Britons talk so much about the weather is that so many outdoor activities depend on it and yet, in its extremes of hot and cold and wet and dry, it is more unpredictably eccentric than almost anywhere else. In the USA, for example, where conditions can be more severe, everyone is equipped to deal with extremes of hot and cold. In Britain, heat waves are crises and prolonged falls of snow are emergencies. It is as though that optimism which traditionally served the population so well during two world wars is also proof against climatic depredations. So inveterate outdoor sportsmen and holiday-makers venture out as cheerfully in winter as in summer and thus occasionally find a serenity in their surroundings that delights the eye and warms the heart. Warming the hands is a different problem – rubber gloves may be worn for wind-surfing, but there is no alternative to bare fingers for eating fish and chips from a newspaper, whilst enjoying the wintry view from the seafront. On both the southwest coast and its marginally less friendly counterpart in the northeast, both kinds of people can be found, usually exhibiting all the signs of enjoying

Windsurfers at Weston-super-Mare (above centre and facing page top right) seem to spend as much time contemplating the waves as riding them. The harbour at Whitby (top left and facing page bottom) is dominated by the old abbey. From the harbour the local fishermen (facing page top left) set out to net the catch that others will later enjoy, with chips, on the seafront (left). Remaining pictures: Scarborough exhibits all the emptiness of a seaside resort out of season.

themselves.

Weston-super-Mare, on the Bristol Channel, is one of those out-and-out Victorian creations, a seaside resort fashioned round an old fishing village. In 1800 its population was less than a hundred; today it has an electoral roll of almost 80,000. There is nothing outwardly elegant about its appearance, but the facilities for enjoyment are extensive and the ooze that is revealed when the tide is at its lowest is reported to exude a particularly health-giving species of ozone. By contrast, St Ives, almost the westernmost of England's seaside towns, has ancient beginnings and a distinguished later history. It is named after St Ia who, in the same way as St Columba came to Scotland, is

Left: a bleak winter outlook at St Ives, Cornwall and (below) Scarborough glowing in glorious winter sunshine. Bottom: the old fishermen's cottages in Whitby go down to the shore in tiers.

said to have arrived from Ireland in a rudimentary boat in the sixth century and to have built a chapel on the headland. One pretender to the English throne, Perkin Warbeck (1474-99), landed nearby in 1498 and the people of St Ives proclaimed him king, an error of judgment that may have influenced their later decision not to back the only royal horse in the race at the time of the Civil War. While the towns around were solidly for Charles I, St Ives supported Parliament. John Wesley (1703-91), founder of the Methodist Church, found a good number of converts in St Ives, some of whose streets commemorate his success in names such as Teetotal Place and Salubrious Place. The town was a leader of the Cornish pilchard fishing industry in the nineteenth century and a port that prospered through traffic in tin and copper. It was saved from the oblivion that engulfed other ports with the decline of these traditional industries by the discovery that its light is particularly good for painting by. It has thus retained its picturesque nature while sheltering ever since a thriving artists' colony.

Scarborough, on the North Yorkshire coast, was originally the site of one of the five Roman signal stations positioned on the cliffs in this area. The town is said to have been founded by Vikings and, in 1066, it was also burned down by a Viking, Harald Hardrada (1015-66), who was then slain at Stamford Bridge by the English King Harold (1022-66). The Normans built a great castle on the headland, some of which still stands, having survived the depredations of the Cromwellians during the Civil War. Its distinction as a spa town came early. A Mrs Farrow claimed, in the middle of the seventeenth century, that water from a stream which flowed across the sands not only had cleansing properties, but would help to cure asthma, jaundice, leprosy, scurvy and also depression. People have been going to Scarborough for their holidays ever since, though sadly Anne Brontë (1820-49), youngest of the three novelist sisters, did not survive one of her frequent visits, dying there of consumption. She is buried in the churchyard of St Mary's on the hillside beneath the castle. There are fishing festivals to

Top: evening sunlight on Scarborough's South Beach, where a solitary man walks his dogs. Left: the beach at St Ives is equally deserted. The locality's clear light is much favoured by artists, when it's not raining of course (below left). The harbour at Whitby (above) is always busy. The town had a whaling fleet in the eighteenth century and was a leading coal port. Captain James Cook (1728-79), the explorer and navigator, lived here for nine years and learned his seamanship from sailing in the coal ships.

compete in and a cricket festival to enjoy in the summer, but the town is also highly favoured as a conference centre in winter. There is still a medieval area, with a house said to have been stayed in by King Richard III, and an old smugglers' inn. Whitby, some twenty miles up the coast, was another Roman signal station. The town also has two claims to a place in ecclesiastical history. St Hild, or Hilda (614-80), abbess of Hartlepool, founded Whitby Abbey in 658 as a monastery for both monks and nuns. The abbey was destroyed by the Danes in 867, was finally abandoned under the Dissolution of the Monasteries by Henry VIII and has since been partly blown down by the wind and partly shelled by the Germans in 1914. Yet enough still remains for it to be a spectacular clifftop ruin and a point of easy recognition for sailors. It was in the abbey that the Synod of Whitby met in 664 and committed the English Church to the Roman rather than the Celtic way of thinking. The ruins, and their atmosphere, served Bram Stoker (1847-1912) brilliantly as the setting for part of his novel, *Dracula,* for it is to Whitby that the ship and its ghastly cargo are consigned. The little town is a real place, rather than an artificially created resort, and it still retains both its old charm and something of its former function as a fishing port.

NATIONAL HUNT RACING, CHELTENHAM

If there is anything which especially reflects the British penchant for watching sports out of doors it is National Hunt racing. Any exhilaration that is lost by not actually competing is amply compensated for by viewing the whole contest in safety and by being able to wager on the result. Although the season actually lasts from August to May, just before the Derby, National Hunt racing is regarded as the great sport of winter, when the chill of the air and the greyness of the sky are warmed by the colours, as well as the skills and courage, of the jockeys and by the characters and prowess of the runners. For heroic jumpers are not, like their flat-racing cousins, retired to stud the moment

Facing page: bookies and binoculars, indispensable accompaniments to a day at the races. Between the pre-race parade in the paddock (left) and the walk into the winners' enclosure (top right) is a gruelling ride over the jumps (top left). The result is always of importance to the betting public (above), but seems of little concern to the groundsmen (above centre).

they show promise, but, as geldings, they are raced for season after season. So legendary horses such as Red Rum, Arkle and Desert Orchid delight their faithful following for many years.

A National Hunt jockey is freelance, although he may also be retained by the trainer of a particular stable. Thus in any one day at a particular meeting he may, if he is in demand, wear the colours of several owners. There is always, however, the danger of a fall. The champion jockey John Francome, whose record

of riding 1,138 winners was broken in 1989, received an early warning of the dangers, as he records in his autobiography. 'On my second ride, which was at Cheltenham, I broke my wrist. The combination of a novice jockey on a novice chaser at Cheltenham is the ideal recipe for disaster and we parted company after we had gone for a little more than a mile. ... After breaking my wrist once and my arm twice within the space of four seasons the penny finally dropped and from then on I was tucked up in a ball ready to fall almost before the horse knew when he was going to make a mistake.'

There are two forms of National Hunt racing, the steeplechase, over a set of fences that vary one from another in their height and difficulty, and hurdling, over uniform barriers so constructed that the portion which is being jumped will give if it is hit, in the same way as a hurdle on an athletics track. Unlike flat racing, which is dominated by the richest owners, many of them from abroad, steeplechasing is a sport for small owners too. Even the most famous national races can be, and have been, won by horses bought for a few thousand pounds and trained by the owner in his own

Left: a bookie chalks up the changing odds beside the runners while (below) a fur hat and a glass of champagne help insulate against the cold. Below left: in the stable, alert and ready to go. Bottom: 'And they're off!'

backyard or on his farm. Little Polveir, winner of the 1989 Grand National as a rank outsider, was originally bought by an enthusiast for his army officer son to ride in point-to-point races. Even as a rider, steeplechasing is a sport that can be participated in at many levels, by both sexes and by amateurs as well as professionals. There is also much vicarious excitement to be had by spectators, whether they are in the stands at Aintree or Cheltenham or spattered with mud as they watch from the sidelines at a local point-to-point. The courses in the west country, Exeter, Bath, Taunton and Wincanton, mark the beginning of the season in August and cater especially for holiday-makers. Nearer London are Ascot, where flat races are also run, Kempton Park and Sandown Park. In the south are Fontwell, Plumpton and Folkestone. The Midlands offer Huntingdon, Stratford, Warwick, Nottingham and Leicester and the north has Haydock, Catterick, Hexham, Carlisle, Wetherby and Kelso, as well as Aintree. Aintree not only hosts the Grand National, but also the annual Foxhunters 'Chase. This race, for

Left: HM Queen Elizabeth, the Queen Mother, first lady of National Hunt racing, braves the elements. She is an owner as well as a keen racegoer.

Bookies (above left) set the odds, but punters (above) may still disagree with them and each other over the favourites. Left: one runner gets some last-minute attention before the race from the stable lad, the trainer and the owner.

amateur riders, is over one circuit of the Grand National course and includes all the famous hazards, such as Bechers Brook, the Chair, Valentines and the Canal Turn. Whereas Aintree and the Grand National get most of the publicity, it is the National Hunt Festival at Cheltenham in March that is the real draw of the season's racing for the connoisseur as well as for the ordinary enthusiast of the sport. As Ivor Herbert, himself a jockey and trainer, put it in his book, *Winter's Tale* (1974): 'The title is a treble misnomer like the old Holy Roman Empire in that it is neither National, nor a Hunt, nor any real Festival. But it is, for those professionally involved in the sport, the pinnacle of the season. Owner, individual horse and jockey may be wreathed with more personal glamour for winning a Grand National, but within the profession no meeting bestows half as much kudos as winning at Cheltenham in March'. National Hunt meetings were originally, as the name implies, essentially for hunting men and were ridden by amateurs on hunters. The first National Hunt steeplechase was run in 1860. In 1861 there was a 'National Hunt Steeplechase' at Cheltenham, though the official race of that name was held at Market Harborough. The National Hunt Committee was

established in 1866 to bring some centralised and realistic control to the sport. The committee's main race took place at various venues round the country, including Bristol, Bedford, Sandown Park, Liverpool and Newmarket, before settling for good at Cheltenham in 1911. Entry was confined to amateurs on horses that had never won a recognised race.

The Cheltenham Gold Cup, instituted in 1924, quickly became the high spot of the March meeting. Its

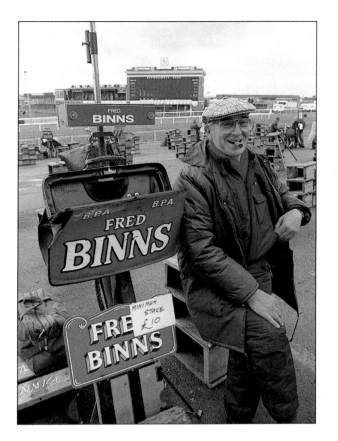

Handicap Chase, the Totalisator Champion Chase and the Champion Hurdle. Thus there is enough variety, as well as prestige and money, on offer to make the event the great occasion it is in the racing calendar. Luck plays a greater part in any race under National Hunt, rather than flat-racing, rules and it can make or destroy a reputation. That is part of the sport's special charm. Yet it is the people who really make it what it is, the officials, the owners, the trainers, the stable lads and girls and the jockeys, as well as the marvellous horses, straining to the limits of their power and endurance, to the excitement of the crowds.

Facing page: discussing form. With a minimum stake of ten pounds, a bookmaker can afford to look genial and smoke cigars (far left). The Sporting Life provides detailed information for punters (left), but the decision is always a personal one. Below: the melee at the start. The state of the turf is a crucial factor in the race and is especially variable in winter. Different conditions suit different horses. Experiments are being conducted at two centres with meetings held on all-weather tracks, the races being run over plastic hurdles.

conditions are different from those of the Grand National in that the course is three and a quarter miles, as opposed to four and a half miles, long and in its handicapping method. Runners in the Grand National are handicapped according to their proven or supposed ability and carry whatever weights the organisers decree. In the Gold Cup the weight each horse carries is calculated strictly according to its age, the youngest horses carrying the least weight. The winner can thus legitimately be regarded as the champion steeplechaser of the year. Although the Gold Cup takes many of the honours, there are three other particular races at Cheltenham to which owners, trainers and jockeys look forward with extra anticipation: the Two Mile

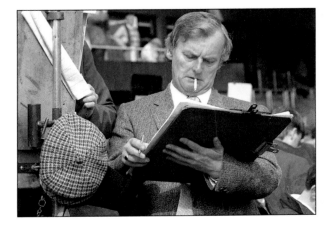

Course bookmakers (left) record all bets taken. Money taken on a particular horse may alter the odds and the process is one of constantly trying to keep the book balanced.

Winter

CALEDONIA, STERN AND WILD

'O Caledonia! stern and wild!' is how Sir Walter Scott (1771-1832) addresses his beloved Scotland in his romantic poem, *The Lay of the Last Minstrel*. The raw grandeur of the Scottish countryside has always evoked deep feelings of darkness and mystery in its inhabitants. During the winter nights, which are that much longer in Scotland than in more southern parts, these feelings grew into beliefs that were expressed round the fireside in the form of stories and incantations. From such beginnings there developed strange customs that the early Christian Church, in its wisdom, did not discourage, but rather incorporated into its own celebrations, grafting a Christian festival onto each existing pagan one. Such was Samhuinn, the Celtic

Facing page: the Inver valley in the northwest Highlands of Scotland looks inviting in the sunshine, but the grip of winter can be severe in this area. Snow dusts the peaks (top left) in the Southern Uplands and (top right) in the Highlands, and (above left) the frozen landscape lends a touch of fairy-tale magic to a manor house at Inveran, Easter Ross. Left: a teacher and her pupils pose beneath a rainbow at Unapool, at the junction of Lochs Cairnbawm, Glendhu, and Glencoul. They constitute the entire village school.

new year festival, which became Hallowe'en, the next day being Hallowmas, the Feast of All Saints, which, in 835, Pope Gregory transferred to 1 November from its original date of 21 February. So, in Scotland, there was an official first day of winter, to which was attached the pagan superstition, 'when Hallowmas is on Wednesday, it is afflictive after it', meaning that it will be a harsh winter. Although Samhuinn appears originally to have been associated with the Cult of the

Dead, it was even in those times not an entirely gloomy occasion, for the seasons symbolised the circle of life. If winter represents death, then the spring that follows it represents resurrection. Certainly the coming of winter on Hallowe'en was hailed with more jollity than any other season of the year.

Hallowe'en is a time for games round the fire, particularly those which involve divination. The white of an egg, dropped into a glass of water, is said to indicate by certain marks how many children a person will have. Apples are especially good for divination rites, captured in the mouth as they swirl round in a bowl or as they swing on the end of a thread. Children go guising, wearing fantastic dress and grotesque masks and carrying turnip lanterns as they go from house to house, performing a dance or suchlike at each one. Hallowe'en used to be thought a time of merriment not only for human but also for supernatural beings. Fairies processed from hill to hill and witches and warlocks sailed through the air or rode around on tabby cats, transformed for the night into coal-black steeds. Or else they would dance shrieking round the churchyard, like those in the poem *Tam o'Shanter*,

Left: a hazy winter sunset over Ullapool, by Loch Broom. Below: the sweep of the Southern Uplands, their bare slopes softened by a covering of snow. Bottom: Ardgay on the Dornoch Firth.

Robert Burns's scary masterpiece of folklore. Ritual bonfires were lit at dusk, originally to combat the powers of darkness, but later to diminish the effect of malevolent influences of all kinds, particularly flying witches. Queen Victoria used to preside at an annual rite at Balmoral in which the effigy of a witch, known as the Shandy Dann, was dragged to the castle and thrown onto the flames.

Martinmas on 11 November is followed by Anermas, or St Andrew's Day, on 30 November, now celebrated more enthusiastically by Scots abroad than those at home, and then by Yule from 25 December to 6 January. Many Christmas customs were transferred to Hogmanay, 31 December, when the celebration of Christmas was banned at the time of the Reformation. Certain traditions still lingered, particularly those associated with food. In humble homes the yule bread was baked. Throughout the Middle Ages, the boar's head was the traditional yuletide dish for the well-to-do in England. In Scotland, however, there existed an ancient Celtic taboo against pork, as a result of which

goose became the Scottish Christmas roast. James VI of Scotland had either an instinctive or a genuine aversion to pork and so, when he came to England as James I, something other than a boar's head had to be found for his Christmas table. Goose smacked too much of Scotland, so recourse was had to the 'jewelled fowl of Mexico', which had just appeared on the gourmet market. It was, of course, the turkey! On Auld Handsel Monday, the first monday after New Year, farm labourers, industrial workers and servants had the day off and received handsels, or gifts, from their employers. Uphalieday was the equivalent of Twelfth Night, celebrated with rowdy games and gargantuan feasts for those who could afford them. The day in the Scottish calendar that is today celebrated with the strictest ritual is in fact a comparatively modern institution. The Burns Supper, which is now held annually in countries all over the world on 25 January, Robert Burns's birthday, was first held in 1859. A further truly Scottish sign of winter is the occasion of a national bonspiel. Curling, or 'the roaring game', as

it is called from the noise the stone makes on the ice, is probably not a Scottish invention, but the national bonspiel, or Grand Match, certainly is. It requires six inches of solid ice before one can be called and, when it is, upwards of 2,500 curling men and women descend on the chosen venue for a day of communal team competition and general rejoicing. There have been only three Grand Matches since the Second World War, at Loch Leven in 1959 and at the Lake of Menteith in 1963 and 1979. The Victorians would not have expected to have to wait more than four years between each occasion, which is the most conclusive evidence that Scottish winters are not as cruel as they used to be, nor the ice so thick. According both to Celtic tradition and to the early Christian Church, winter in Scotland ends on 31 January. The following day is dedicated to St Bride, Christian successor to a Celtic goddess and also, as St Bridget (452-525), the first nun in Ireland. The day after that, 2 February, is Candlemas, when the Scots at least claim that spring is once more under way.

The tiny cemetery of the church at Elphin, on the Cam Loch (top) looks especially bleak in winter. The west Highland coast (above and above left) between Lochinver and Ullapool has a rugged beauty, even under threatening skies. So too have the Highlands (left), where the clouds descend to meet the water.

Overleaf: a typically British downpour at Newmarket races.